HUNGRY FOR HAPPINESS

One woman's journey from fighting food to finding freedom

BY SAMANTHA SKELLY

Hungry for Happiness, San Diego, California
Copyright © 2017 Samantha Skelly

Cover and Interior Design
Lauren Pagan

Editing
Nicole Calla

Author's Photo
Andrew Reed Photography

DEDICATION

For Mom, the original phoenix.

Your resilience, dedication, and courage constantly
gives me full permission to rise.

I love you,
Sammy.

Hungry For Happiness Foreword

If you have told yourself a story that the extra weight you carry is because you have not found the right trainer, gym or diet that works for you, then you're in for an awakening. If you insist on holding onto that story however, then I don't believe this book is for you.

This is a book that will strip away the bullshit and expose the truth about weight loss and weight gain, and get to the core of the real reason why so many of us carry excess weight and find it hard to lose.

There is so much focus on the working out part of the equation and increasingly more on the what we put in our body. When it comes to exploring how emotion plays its part however, it has become the distant cousin and yet I believe it is actually at the very foundation of the real root cause of the problem, and therefore the foundation of the solution.

We have science telling us that this is the perfect workout, television telling us this is the perfect machine and experts telling us this is what you should put in your mouth. Where is the conversation regarding what we need to let go of, or remove? Most people are carrying an emotional backpack with them each and every day. It's filled with big and small rocks that represent unresolved emotions and scars from the past. Many of us are pulled back by our emotional past and pulled down by the masks we wear daily to try and fit in.

It's time to unpack the past and let go of the perfection mask that is so exhausting to wear, it could be made out of steel.

What makes this book so important is not the science, research, exercises or the design of the cover. What makes it important is the story of a real women who is prepared to remove her mask, let down her guard and allow us to enter the scared space of her personal and imperfect narrative. Samantha is not telling you what to do but rather inviting you to question the past so you can free your future. She is showing you a path and inviting you along on your own journey. She is revealing her own personal pain so that you can reconcile your own. She is willing to be vulnerable in order to inspire.

The only question now is: will you step in?

So many people wish they had a different body, a different story and a different result. This lies at the very core of the real issue which is the insanely human need to want what others have. Only by addressing how we really view who we are and its associated cost can we begin the challenging but not impossible journey of self acceptance. God forbid we would ever stop judging ourselves and replace that choice to berate oneself with the 'c' word.

The 'c' word is usually held for others and is something we allow out when we are deeply moved emotionally. Many of us see how and why the 'c' word could and should be used externally to mend bridges and allow people know they matter. Sadly most people walk this earth never fully experiencing the full effects of the 'c' word for and to themselves. I'm referring to not just the word compassion but the gift of compassion that we can absolutely bestow upon ourselves.

Its not until we reach this sacred place can we ever mend the past and be truly at peace with our future.

Thank you Samantha for being courageous enough to write this book and to share your story in the hope of freeing others from theirs.

Philip McKernan
Speaker, Author & Filmmaker

Acknowledgments

I am constantly in awe of how my life plays out on a daily basis. I love looking back seeing how the seemingly insignificant circumstances have turned into the biggest milestones of my life. If I were to name all the souls with whom I've crossed paths who have impacted the creation of Hungry For Happiness, this book would double in size. I've been graciously blessed with incredible humans that have not only crossed my path, but added value to my life and my work in beautiful ways.

My family - where do I even start? I truly couldn't imagine a better family structure, and not a day goes by where I don't feel incredible gratitude for each of you. Our home was always so full of love, laughter, dreams, and embracing the impossible. Mom, Dad, and Chris - thank you for supporting all my crazy ideas, thank you for saying 'yes' to me, and thank you for believing in me when I couldn't believe in myself. Dad - you're my best friend, my hero, and my greatest inspiration. Your humour, compassion, and dedication to excellence are some of my greatest teachers. Mom - you constantly amaze me with your grace, commitment to serve, and beautiful heart. You are the greatest mom in the world. Chris - thank you for being my rock throughout my childhood. You played such a vital role in my life, were incredibly supportive, and always had my back. I still don't forgive you for not allowing me to date your friends, but I'll get over it one day. I am so proud of the person you've become in this world. Britt - I love you like a sister. Welcome to the family.

Dad & Jodi - it's rare a child is blessed with one set of incredible parents, but I am so honoured I have two. You both have been unwavering in your support, always being there for me, supporting my crazy adventures, and welcoming me home as if I never left. I am so honoured and grateful to have you both as parents. Thank you for everything you do for me.

To all my mentors and coaches - thank you for seeing me, thank you for pushing me to the edge, for not letting me waver and get off course. Knowing I have you on in my corner to push me, strengthen me, and empower me gives me incredible wings. Ray Williams, Shannon Graham, Philip Mckernan, and Neil Moore: thank you, thank you, thank you!

My silly, outrageous, beautiful friends - I love how I can be fully, unapologetically expressive around you guys and all you do is laugh with me. Thank you for the dance parties, the slip and slide adventures, the taco eating extravaganzas, the epic, spur of the moment travels, the jokes, the heart-to-hearts, and all the paloozas. You all are up to huge things in the world, and it's inspiring to grow alongside you.

Jenn (a.k.a. Snazzie) - You're not just my right hand; you are my front, back, and both sides. Your support towards me and your thirst for our mission is what truly fuels Hungry For Happiness. I thank God each and everyday that you were brought to me in such a divine fashion. Dreaming and creating with you is not only fun, it's changing the world. I love you.

My tribe of Phoenixes. You amazing women give me purpose, you fuel me to keep showing up each and every day and serving you from my highest self. Thank you for trusting me, doing the work, and contributing to the community. Together we will ignite the world and help others break free from the battle with food and their bodies.

Finally, thank you to you, the beautiful soul reading this book. I trust the words on the paper will ignite something inside of you to become the highest, best, and most authentic version of yourself.

I love you,
Samantha

TABLE OF CONTENTS

INTRODUCTION

This book is for women who want to reclaim their power.
This book is for women who want to say "fuck it" to dieting.
This book is for women who know they were designed for more.
This book is for women who want to end their battle with food.
This book is for women who are craving joy.
This book is for women who want to feel alive again.

Our relationship with food is a blessing.

I know you're thinking, "Sam, that's not true. My fight with food is eating me alive, literally."

Yes, I know. My fight with food ate me alive, too. I lived in a "diet depression" for years of my life, and you're right, it's a battle – a constant war in your mind. There were days I wanted to crawl out of my skin and into a hole to hide away from the world. I had a voice in my head that didn't shut up, no matter how much I tried to distract myself with puppy videos on Facebook or over-exercising. I get you, girl. I get all of you. I see you. I feel you. I was you.

We are one. Your struggle is my struggle; my freedom is your freedom. We are on this journey together: co-existing, growing, and expanding into the highest, best, and most authentic versions of ourselves.

You're searching for a remedy, an escape, an answer to the battle you've created in your mind. You are looking for a "get out of jail free" card from the vicious cycle you're in with food and your body. This book is it. This is your answer.

I want you to know something, my fellow warrior: the battle you're in is temporary. The battle you're in is soon going to become the catalyst to your growth, and it will soon become a blessing. The universe knew you could handle it, that at your core, you are a perfect, abundant being so capable of overcoming your issues with food and your body. I promise you that you haven't been given anything you can't handle.

You are a wise woman, but your logical mind has gotten the better of you.

You've been over-thinking, over-analysing, and banging your head against a wall, trying to figure out how to just eat like a normal person. Here's the thing: brain power will not break you out of this. You can't think your way out of your fight with food. You need to feel. You need to feel in order to heal.

When we are dieting, we run away from our bodies and take action out of fear. We hate how we look, so we jump on the next miracle diet in a desperate attempt to reach the ideal image we have of ourselves. Then, when we give up because we can't possibly sustain such restrictive behaviours, we tell ourselves we have no will power and that we are failures at life. Sound about right?

It's time to revolutionize the way you release weight. Physical weight on your body is often a representation of the emotional weight you are carrying. Weight loss is an emotional issue and can't be sustained by restricting calories or spending a few more hours in the gym. We have to treat emotional problems with emotional solutions. We need to get into our bodies and heal at our core so we are no longer victims to the madness in our minds.

Hungry For Happiness will open your mind and crack open your heart. This book will provide you the clarity you are craving for your foggy and frustrated mind. It will ease the frustration, speak to your struggle, and show you how to break free from your battle. I want you to get down and dirty when you implement the strategies I present in this book. Do the work and shift the emotional heaviness that is showing up on your heart and on your body. Then, and only then, will you be able to create sustainable transformation in your mind and body.

I've worked with hundreds of women in countries all over the world who are desperately looking for peace with food. Many of these women believed they had to no chance in hell of ever loving their bodies or using food for health and hunger. I've spoken on stages around the world sharing my process of helping women break free of this cycle. I teach this process in my group programs and on my retreats, and now I get to share it with you in the pages of this book.

I know it will open your mind, crack open your heart, and allow you to explore the depths of your soul. My philosophy is that weight loss needs to be a result of doing the emotional work, not the focus. My mission is to revolutionize the weight loss industry by teaching women to dig into what they're actually hungry for, healing their emotional bodies first. When we are tuned into our bodies, rather than numbing our emotions with food, we can use our awareness as a catalyst for growth.

Suffering is learned behavior; it's not innate within us. We are fundamentally designed to be happy. We are fundamentally designed to have lightness in our minds and in our bodies. Pain is mandatory. Suffering is optional. We prolong our suffering when we believe we don't have the ability to transform. We wait, we make excuses, and we self-sabotage. We beat around the bush and throw obstacles in our way, which distance us from living our truth. Why? Because there is a small part of us that believes we don't deserve happiness.

Jump into this book with both feet. Allow me to not only catch you, but guide you. Come on a journey with me — a journey back into your body to reclaim your abundant power.

This is your chance. See you inside.

You've got this.

MY PERSONAL HELL
Chapter 1

153 pounds.

You are worthless. You have no willpower.
You will never be skinny, so why even bother?

My scale told me how worthy I was. The way my clothes fit told me if I was loveable or not. My calorie intake told me how much strength I had.

I sat in my London apartment sipping Earl Grey tea while flipping through Women's Health magazine. The steam from the tea fogged my glasses, masking the tears rolling down my face. My chest was tight as I flipped through the magazine on a desperate search for my next diet. It was Sunday night at 9:34 pm – crunch time. I needed to find the next diet, lock it in, and shop for it before 10:00 pm. I looked down at my food journal from the weekend, and I was overcome with shame, guilt, and fear as I frantically searched through the magazine for my miracle diet.

"Lean and Mean" splashed across the page in bright pink letters with a photo of a woman who resembled a Victoria's Secret model. This will do, I thought as I ripped out the diet, threw on my jacket and b-lined for the nearest grocery store. Tears still rolling down my face, I had the torn magazine page in one hand and my wallet in the other. I entered the store, and the blast of cold air and the smell of fresh bread welcomed me. As I tried to ignore the calls of fresh bread, I read the list of diet appropriate foods, and with a pit in my stomach, I sauntered around the grocery store and picked out the foods that were acceptable. Boring as fuck, I thought.

I made my way back to my flat and unpacked the groceries. I decided that week I needed to lose six pounds, and I could definitely do it by Friday night. I calculated how many calories I was going to eat and how many calories I was going to burn to create enough of a deficiency in my body to lose those pounds. My strategic brain was activated as my heart sank.

I posted the diet plan on the fridge to remind me to keep on track. The Victoria's Secret model stared at me right in the eyes each time I opened the fridge. Knowing I was about to intensely restrict my diet, I decided to have one last hurrah and inhale a few spoonfuls of peanut butter. I put the peanut butter back in the fridge and went right for the scale.

153.4 pounds.

I sighed as I calculated my goal weight for the week.
147.4 pounds by Friday. I can force through this. It's only five days.

I grabbed my schedule and carefully planned my workouts. Ninety minutes each day, with at least an hour of intense cardio - anything less than that and I'd immediately label myself as weak. These commitments were non-negotiable. I had everything calculated to the last detail it was a mathematical masterpiece.

Being a woman of intentional goal setting, I laid down on my bed and wrote out my goals for the week:

Lose six pounds.

Follow diet to a tee - only 1000 calories a day.
Workout every day - 90 minutes.
Absolutely no sugar or alcohol.

That was it. No problem, right?

I dusted off my journal, drank my final sip of lukewarm tea, switched off the light, and went to bed.

This was my life. Day after day after day. For years. I lived my own personal hell, my own personal battle – self-created, self-perpetuated.

My personal hell began at a young age. I grew up as a dancer while working in the film industry. When I wasn't on a stage, I was in front of a camera. My body was always under a microscope. I strived for perfection: in my performance and in my body. I was also held to a high level of perfectionism by my agents, who banked on my looks for booking gigs.

When I was 18, I threw in the towel on my dance career as well as my acting career. It was in that moment when I became ruthlessly obsessed with the relationship I had with food and my body. I took off to Australia with my best friend, Maria, for a year to go away and find ourselves.

Because I'd stopped dancing, I was terrified of blowing up to 300 pounds. To ensure this didn't happen, I began restricting my calories.

It was innocent at first. I simply masked my new behavior as healthy eating, which is the easiest excuse to cover up the fact you're terrified of gaining weight. After all, healthy eating is celebrated on the regular; so really, my dysfunctional way of eating was constantly praised. I was told I was committed, hardworking, and dedicated to my health.

Until I ended up in the hospital.

On June 16, 2008, I found myself in a hospital in Cairns with tubes coming out of my body. I was severely malnourished. Months of skipping meals and not eating properly led to severe stomach pains and hospitalization. The story I told myself was I was simply saving money as a budget-wise traveler. Looking back, it was a pretty good story. Believable to some, I suppose.

The truth of the matter was I was hiding the biggest secret of my life: the fact I was in a terrible fight with food. As far as I was concerned, food was the enemy, so I lived in a constant state of deprivation. Depriving myself of the essential nutrients for survival, I thought I could outsmart my body. My body fought back in a hard way, internally paining me to the point of hospitalization.

I learned my lesson, for a few weeks. I ate properly, didn't count calories, and relaxed knowing I needed to refuel my body. Those were the doctor's orders, and I listened.

I listened until fear overcame me again, and I decided that three meals a day just wasn't necessary. I did whatever I needed to do to justify this to myself. I tuned out the intensity of the doctor's voice; I distracted myself with going back to counting calories and restricting. It felt comfortable and safe.

Eating more than what I allowed myself terrified me. Even if I were 100 calories over my daily allowance, I would do whatever I could to ensure that 100 calories didn't show up on my body. If I overate, I'd find out how many jumping jacks I needed to do to immediately burn it off; I didn't feel safe until I knew, for certain, I burned it off. Even after I burned it off, I would still carry the guilt and shame of overeating.

Why can't you just be strong?

If you can't even do something as simple as not eat, how are you supposed to have a relationship? You're such a failure.

Still, for me - this felt safe. Safe, exhausting, and debilitating. I didn't trust myself to eat reasonably like a normal person. I didn't know what that felt like. I was so deep in my shame cycle, deep in my disconnection, deep in my self-created hell, I had no idea how to even breathe, let alone eat properly.

I designed my perfect little hell in my mind.

I've always been a fantastic storyteller. (I really should have stuck with the whole acting thing.) I could tell the story of "I'm fine" all day long, all the while telling myself the story of "I'm not enough" at the same time. It takes some serious skill to be able to pull that off with ease.

The conversation in my mind was the exact opposite of the conversion I was having with people around me. And funnily enough, those people who knew me at that time still don't quite believe what happened. I put on a damn good show, day after day after day. It was the most exhausting show I've ever had to put on.

I am also naturally an extremely creative person. I thought of every excuse in the book as to why I couldn't come to that social event, or eat that piece of cake. I was a fountain of endless excuses, which all supported the carefully crafted story I created.

This story held me captive for years; I was so consumed with the story, I couldn't live any other way. This was the only way that made sense to me. The fear that came up when I thought of anything else was too much to bear, so the deception continued.

Three years later, I was living in London. My chai latte felt warming and comforting as I walked down Oxford Street. The gentle taste of the spice with almond milk was the most comforting sensation I had felt all day. My beautiful mother always made chai tea on rainy Vancouver days. I would come home from school, and she would be over the stove whisking the carefully crafted creation, knowing it was my favorite remedy on a cold day.

Not living in the same city with my mom was a challenge. She is my safe place - I can tell her everything. I even distanced myself from her during this time, because she saw right through my stories. I can't get away with anything with her. As a teenager, I tried to lie to her about "sleeping at Carly's" when really, I was at my boyfriend's house, and it never worked. I'd immediately start laughing. We are incredibly in tune with one another.

As I continued down Oxford Street, I window shopped in some of the most iconic stores on earth. As I passed Selfridges, Topshop, and Victoria's Secret, I immediately started planning my Monday diet. It was Saturday — it was always Saturday when I started to think about the week's diet. Guilt overcame me as I remembered what I had eaten the night before, not to mention the multiple glasses of wine, which resulted in binge eating even more. One glass of wine, and I lost all inhibitions. This was the pattern.

I looked on Instagram and searched #celebritydiets, because of course celebrities know it all. I found a diet I'd already done three times in the last year, but this time I was going to just do it again, do it harder, because obviously, last time I didn't have enough willpower.

I finished my chai latte, and distracted myself with some mindless shopping. Fighting crowds and getting frustrated, I jumped on the underground and took the Northern Line to Clapham where I lived. Sweaty and disheveled, I climbed the stairs from the tube station into the grocery store. I pulled up the link, and awkwardly juggled my bags as I tried to read the list of acceptable and forbidden foods, which of course was wildly different from last week. All greens and proteins, the celebs swore by this one.

My meal prep for the week looked like I was prepping snacks for a baby rabbit. Tasteless and lacking substance. This was my life.

Monday morning I got a text from Hannah, one of my best friends living in London.

"Sam, dinner and drinks tonight in Covent Garden. Let's hit up that French place."

My heart sank and my throat got tight. There was no way I could go for dinner. It wasn't part of the plan. It wasn't on the list. There would be no way I could modify everything on the menu to suit my specific dietary needs, plus that would not only be embarrassing, but a total waste of an experience. I hadn't seen Hannah in three weeks, which was record breaking. We were attached at the hip.

"Can't tonight, love, I've got plans."

Plans, yes Sam. Plans to stay in and be miserable, plans to sit there in the thick of your shit feeling so sorry for yourself that you've decided to stay in because you're terrified of getting fat. You are seriously an idiot. Not to mention a fucking liar.

Hannah didn't resist. She just accepted graciously and said we needed to meet up soon. After sending that text, I tossed my iPhone in my bag and headed out the door to work. I jumped on the tube full of sweaty, miserable humans and headed into the core of London. I worked in a beautiful and quaint part of the city called Marylebone, where the rich, super rich, and stupidly rich people lived and hung out.

I got off the train and headed to the insanely posh hair salon I managed. I managed a team of 30 hairdressers – yes, diva central. This environment only reinforced my disorder. The clients and staff were constantly talking about dieting and losing that extra ten pounds.

I threw my bag on the desk in my office and locked the door. I sat down in my chair and let out the biggest sigh. I counted on two minutes of peace before someone was knocking on my door explaining their latest drama to me. I opened my bag and pulled out two boiled eggs, half a cucumber, and a few bags of shit tea. Yes, that is a thing. Tea that literally makes you shit your pants to lose weight. I drank this by the gallon. When I wasn't choking down tasteless food, I was drowning my body in laxative tea. After all, I was in England, where drinking tea was a way of life – they weren't specific as to what kind of tea to drink. I took it upon myself to make that decision.

I unlocked the door and headed to the kitchen to get some boiling water, and I steeped this bad boy for as long as I needed to in order to get the shit effects as potent as possible. I sat back down at my desk and opened my calorie counter app. I added in the tea - even though it was zero calories. I did it just to feel good about myself for a split second.

So far, so good, I thought as I opened my computer and tried to busy my mind with something other than my disgusting obsession with food and my body. It was 8:30 am, and my mind was already exhausted with mental anguish – I craved even just one moment of clarity, one moment where I could feel happy in my body. These moments were rare. It was impossible to penetrate the war zone I created inside the confines of my own mind. I had to force myself to focus on anything else. I felt the need to slap my face to interrupt the thought pattern. I needed to make my body feel pain to snap me out for a split second.

I wanted to scream, run far away, and never come back. I wanted to escape my mind, leave it behind, and find myself on a beach where my destructive thoughts and behaviors didn't ruin my life.

I felt trapped at all times - if I took a moment to pause or reflect, the mere intensity of my thoughts and feelings would drive me insane, so I kept busy, every moment of the day. I was always looking for ways to distract myself from feeling and being in the present moment. Who knew what I would find if I just for a moment let my shoulders relax and took a deep breath? If I stopped to dig into something emotional, would I be able to handle it? Would I be able to deal with what arose? I wasn't confident I would be. The thought of uncovering a childhood wound was an idea I just wasn't willing to entertain, so I made sure I had a bank of distractions ready to use at all times.

I had created this reality for myself. A living hell within the confines of my own mind. A place where everything was darker, heavier, and depressing. If only people could see the difference between my shining exterior and my dark interior. You're a fraud, I thought. The lack of integrity between how I felt and how I showed up in the world was eating me alive, literally.

Leaving work one day, I thought about my life and wondered if I would ever get back to myself. I missed myself; I missed the optimistic girl who was always in love with life and everyone around her.

Here I was, halfway around the world, in a job that was eating my soul, in a city that gave me anxiety and in the most unhappy relationship of my life. I moved across the world for a boy who I was once deeply in love with, and now, the thought of having sex with him made me sick to my stomach, to the point where I'd just pretend I was sleeping to avoid it at all costs.

I continued to walk down the street, reached into my bag for my phone, and called my mom. I knew as I was reaching into my pocket that I was about to have a meltdown in the middle of the street in London, I felt the emotional pooling in my throat. Whenever I'm feeling even the slightly bit sad, I call my mom. All my emotions intensify and I turn into a sobbing disaster, every single time.

I mustered up the strength to say, "Hey, Mom," and right away, she knew.

"Baby, is everything ok?"

I lost it.

I dropped my bags down on the side of the street, squatted down with my hands in my face and just bawled my eyes out. Londoners were making their evening commutes and just strolled past me: classic Londoner reaction.

I told her how my life was completely falling apart, and I failed to mention the whole part about food and my body. I strategically left that information out.

"Honey, I think it's time to come home."

I knew she was right. I knew I needed to get back to Vancouver and finally heal myself, heal my relationship to food – get myself out of the hole I'd been digging for the last four years. I was longing to feel like myself again. I completely lost myself, and I was terrified I would never be able to find the real me again.

PRACTICE IN ACTION

When most people are trying to change and transform, they start from a place of fear. They hate their bodies and they take drastic action essentially to run away from their bodies.

When we finally get there — wherever there happens to be — we throw in the towel and go back to where we started, feeling more defeated, more overwhelmed, and more like a failure.

I repeated this pattern 50 times in less than four years. It's almost embarrassing to admit. What I never once considered was what I truly wanted, how I wanted to feel.

Let's be real. We are searching for a feeling, not a size. As you go through this book, I want you to treat it like a workbook. I don't want you to read this book and for it to become shelf help — you know — collecting dust as you binge on Oreos. That is not what we are doing.

I want you to dig your teeth into this book, use all the strategies, and get the most out of it. I can promise, if you follow the exercises and give it your all, you will see a drastic change in your relationship with food.

It's time to burn the bridges and commit.

Are you ready?

EXERCISE #1

I want you to visualize yourself in six months' time.

Where do you want to be?
How do you want to feel?
Who do you want to become?

I want you to get crystal clear with this version of you; we need to create it clearly in the mind. What we create in the mind we create in reality; this is a critical part of this journey.

Do not skip this step. You're not above it. Trust me. I do this exercise each time I want to shift a habit or level up in some area. I always get on the other side of it, which means I feel what it feels like to already have it. Our subconscious mind does not know the difference.

Write a letter from your future self to who you are today, explaining how life is different, how you feel in your body and how much mental energy you have to focus on the things you love, rather than fighting food.

When you've finished writing the letter, pop over to the Phoenix Tribe and let us know. Accountability is key. I want to hear from you.

MANTRA

I am worthy and deserving of becoming the highest, best, and most authentic version of myself.

MY DIET DEPRESSION
Chapter 2

I was an actor.

Of course, I was good at telling stories.

No, not good. Exceptional.

I told myself, and everyone around me, a story of how well I was doing. Despite the fact I was living in a constant battle, I still showed up as this beacon of health, light, and love. I struggled in silence and faced the demons, which made themselves comfortable in my mind and body.

I'm not quite sure how I so effectively developed this skill of secrecy, considering when I was a child I couldn't keep a secret to save my life. Something switched within my diet depression that allowed me to sneak around and keep this debilitating behaviour a secret from the people in my life who meant the most to me.

I felt the need to be in control of everything in my life. I spun ten plates in the air at once, praying they wouldn't crash all over the floor. I was living on the edge of desperation in every moment. I walked around in fear feeling at any moment, I was going to be found out, and I'd have to confess. Coming clean with those around me was the very thing I feared the most – telling Hannah I cancelled our plans, not because I was busy, but because I was on a diet and didn't want to break it. How would people respond? What would people think of me?

I continued to tell this story each and every day. I was fantastic at rationalizing my behavior. I knew what I was doing was destructive and

ruining my life, but I had the ability to tell myself that it was okay.
It won't be like this forever... just stick with it until you reach your goal...
everything will be better without these last 10 pounds...just fight through...
you're almost there.
It was Thursday: day four of the diet.

I stood in my kitchen staring at a jar of Nutella. Of course, the deliciously
smooth chocolate was definitely not on the list of foods I was allowed, but
the cucumber and egg combo I was supposed to have for dinner didn't
hold a candle to the Nutella.

I tossed the warm egg and cucumber in the garbage and grabbed the
Nutella and a spoon. I sat myself on my couch with a glass of wine and ate
the rest of the Nutella.

I was in a trance. I felt like I was high on drugs. I couldn't stop eating – I
couldn't speak or even think clearly. It was as if my body was there, but my
mind was absent – something outside of me took over. I was on a mission:
I had to destroy the jar of Nutella.

Moments after my mission was complete, I sunk deeper into the couch and
immediately felt that pang of guilt that I could count on like clockwork as
soon as I had a binge. My body was simultaneously dealing with an intense
sugar hit and a wave of debilitating guilt. The combination was paralyzing.

I sat there staring at the empty jar of Nutella. I grabbed the half-drunk glass
of wine and took a few sips in a desperate attempt to quell the guilt I felt.

The dialogue taking place in my mind was awful – the words were hitting
me like knives, and I felt every ounce of my worth dissipate as shame
swept over me. My palms were sweaty, my heart was racing, and my face
was inflamed. I marinated in this pain, feeling it fully until it was too much
to bear.

I got up, put on my Nikes, and ran until I felt like I was going to vomit. It was
a cold, drizzly day in London, and the air burned my ears while the rain
pierced my skin. I didn't care. No amount of physical pain could override
the emotional pain I was experiencing. I could have been shot in the foot
and not have felt it.

I could feel the tension of my anxiety through the physical pain from running hard for 60 minutes. I was running away from my body, away from my pain, away from my reality.

This wasn't a special occasion. This wasn't a one-time thing. This was a normal occurrence in the world of my diet depression; it was as normal as going out for drinks with the girls or watching re-runs of Homeland. I wish I could say I slipped up and this only happened once or twice, but that would be a complete and utter lie. This was the shameful behaviour I hid from the world and never spoke about. This was just another day in my life.

I wore the struggle as a badge of honour, because it was something that made me feel like I had purpose. The thought of not struggling was almost as painful as being in the struggle.

If I didn't struggle, what would I obsess about?

I brought myself back to just four years earlier, when I simply used food for health and hunger, when my body wasn't the enemy. I wondered what I did with all my energy, all my mental space, because right now, the battle with food and my body was taking up 90% of my mental bandwidth.

Growing up with two parents who were exceptional cooks, every evening was a gourmet meal. We were never a chicken and rice kind of family. Dad was always preparing incredible concoctions while mom finely chopped ingredients most people had never heard of. There was so much love that surrounded food, it was respected and enjoyed with love and presence. Each night the four of us would sit down, pray together, bless the foods our bodies were about to receive, and enjoy the beautifully crafted meal together. I rarely missed this sacred time, unless I was at dance class, in which case dad would always make me a plate and leave it in the fridge for when I came home.

I loved watching my mom's face light up when she explained how she made everything, as she took such great joy in preparing delicious food to feed us. My mom was the mom everyone wanted, and all my friends always wanted to come hang out at my parents' house because my mom and dad were so incredible. When I would bring friends home from school, there mom would be, in the kitchen stirring a beautiful pot of homemade soup with fresh bread baking in the oven. She was a lovely nurturer who took great pride in her role as a mother, and still does to this day.

I remember thinking about how easy it was to eat when I was younger, before my diet depression. I savored, connected with, and enjoyed my food. I was able to have conversations, be present, and stop when I was full – there was an ease to the whole experience. In the thick of my disordered eating, I could barely even remember what a positive relationship with food was like, let alone try to get back to it – I deemed that as impossible. I was going to be in this struggle for the rest of my life.

I turned into an addict. I was addicted to the consumption as well as the restriction of food. Food for me was my drug of choice: socially acceptable and easy to hide from other people. I was able to get away with my addiction without anyone really questioning me for nearly five years of my life. Nutella was the answer to every little bit of discomfort I felt in my body.

"Just one scoop," I'd say to myself, as I stood on my tippy toes reaching for the jar. I would intentionally place it somewhere high in a fruitless attempt to keep myself from it, but that never worked. I had already made up my mind before I went into the kitchen.

I was so emotionally attached to food, so much so that it took over my whole life. I couldn't leave the house without preparing what I was (or was not) going to eat that day. If I decided that I'd let myself eat, I would always have snacks in my bag, because I feared being hungry (when I wasn't restricting). It really made no sense at all.

All my decisions were based in fear. None of it came from a place of love or what I intuitively knew was best for my body. I was run by fear, everything I did was because I was scared of getting fat. I threw myself under the bus repeatedly, because I didn't have the self-love or self-trust to treat myself well. I was terrible to myself, in a way I would never dream of treating anyone else or allow anyone else in the world treat me.

I remember one day when I sat at the dining room table with a plate of fruit in front of me. I sat there with a cup of shit tea and stared at the fruit. Earlier that day, I had watched a YouTube video on mindful eating. I wrote down the lessons from the clip and decided to try it.
I did exactly what the video told me to do: stare at the food and just breathe. I took breath after breath trying to calm my body down, but I couldn't. I felt an uncontrollable impulse just to inhale the food and get onto the next thing.

I fought it and I fought it. I smacked my elbow down on the table and hid my face in my palm.

This is fucking impossible! I thought as I stared at the food. My emotions were raging. They were getting stronger and stronger with each breath, and the intensity was debilitating. Tears started to roll off my face and onto the table, while I prayed my housemates wouldn't come in as I was in the middle of this battle.

I pushed the plate away cradled my face with both my hands and balled my eyes out. I was overcome with pain and frustration. I desperately tried to imagine myself as a child, sitting at the table with my family eating food, just as we had done for years. That feeling was incredibly distant – it was simply just a memory. There was no visceral feeling attached to it anymore. It almost felt like that 15-year-old girl wasn't even me.

I closed my eyes and imagined my mom in the kitchen of our house. I knew all the Neuro-Linguistic Programming tricks like the back of my hand.

If I just imagine myself in a place where I'm not struggling then blend the reality, and...POOF! It will all work.

Nope. I outsmarted even this NLP. I focused on my 15-year-old self. I started asking her questions like, "How did you just eat like a normal person?" or "How can I love my body?" in hopes the answers would be crystal clear and I would just get on with my life. All I wanted was to know how to handle these emotions and not try to diet myself out of them. I tried to imagine my life with this struggle for the rest of my life. I didn't see a way out of it, so I needed to create my life around it.

At this point, I wanted to be a TV celebrity personal trainer, flying all over the world and training celebrities. I could feel the "fraud" sticker painted on my head as I tried to imagine this reality: there was no way I could follow this dream while I was living my own painful reality. I craved consistency; all I wanted was to feel on the outside as I did on the inside. There was a drastic difference.

It terrified me to ruin my image of being "the happy optimistic one", "the funny one", or the one that has all her "poop in a group". The one that never seems to have a bad day. The interesting thing is, I know these are my natural states, I know I've always been this way.

Instead of embracing my natural optimistic state, I created a lingering sadness in my body that frightened me. I obsessed over it, tried to push it away, and wronged myself for having it. But, I discovered that fighting it only strengthened it.

I scoured the internet for blogs to get rid of sadness.

"This isn't me!" I screamed out to my computer screen in a desperate attempt to find the answer. Every blog I read told me simply to accept the sadness, and it will dissipate. This seemed ridiculous to me. In my mind, it made logical sense to fight it and suppress it. Eventually it would go away.

It's just a phase, I would tell myself on a regular basis in a desperate attempt to make myself feel better.

Surely, I am not going to be stuck like this for life. Right?

Rather than making the decisive decision that I was not going to struggle with this battle for my whole life, I created my life around the battle, which kept me chained to the struggle.

When we create our lives around the battle, we wrap our significance in the struggle. Wait. What?

Feeling significant is a human need. All human beings must feel like they have some purpose, some way of being important. They can meet this need for significance in a negative way, like someone who decides to take a gun to school. Alternatively, they can meet it in a very positive way like someone who decides to dedicate their life to building wells in Africa.

Those are two extreme examples, but of course, we can find something in between that will satisfy our need to feel significant.

While I was in the depths of my struggle, I had no idea this was even a thing. A year before this, I was at a Tony Robbins conference and he was banging on about the need for significance, but not once during my diet depression did I consider my battle was a cry for significance. It wasn't until the fog had lifted years later I was really able to see into this.

Humans are addicted to their need for significance. A lot of the time, we create things in our lives so we have something that makes us feel significant. We do things to meet that need, and a lot of the time the things we do are not aligned with who we truly are – it's a desperate attempt to feel something, anything.

We are emotionally driven beings, meaning we take action in an attempt to feel a desired sensation. Feeling like I was significant made me feel like I was important, as if I had something to deal with. My battle was my significance.

What I failed to consider during this period was that I was in complete control of my beliefs. My beliefs shaped my life, and within each moment, I had the power and ability to shift my beliefs to yield a different result. I was not a victim. Life was not doing this to me. I was creating the struggle myself.

I anchored myself in thoughts, which were not serving the highest version of myself, so my mind would search incessantly for evidence as to why these thoughts were true. My mind was constantly collecting data to validate my belief that "I'm not deserving" and it presented the evidence each day. What I didn't take into consideration was that I could choose differently – I could fundamentally choose a different belief that would yield a different result. I was in hyper victim mode, thinking that everything was happening to me, no one has it as bad as I do, and no one understands me. All of this was a result of my core beliefs.

We always have the power of choice in this life. In each moment we can choose any number of emotions – we always have the ability to pivot, to alter, and to shift our inner states to see the world differently. If only I had known I had this power in the thick of my diet depression!

When we shift our core beliefs, we shift our thoughts, which evoke a different feeling in our bodies. When we feel differently, we act differently, therefore changing our lives. It all starts from a place of choice: making a decisive decision that you are going to raise your standards and become the highest and most authentic version of you.

PRACTICE IN ACTION

I had stories about how I would never get over my fight with food. I deemed it impossible. I literally thought to myself on a regular basis,

Cool! This is me. This was the hand I was dealt.
I am just going to suffer for life.

I never thought there would be an end to my obsession. What was holding me back wasn't the behaviours, but the stories I told myself about the behaviours.

I had strong stories about my relationship to food:

I don't have the willpower to get over this.
It's been too long. I'm stuck like this for life.
I've tried everything to get over this.
No one understand me. I'm a freak.

I had to get super clear with the stories I was running in my head on a regular basis. It was impossible for me to shift them if I had no idea what they were.

EXERCISE #2

Set a timer for ten minutes and write down all the stories you have around food and your body. Essentially, I want you to dump all of your subconscious thoughts on the page so you can observe them. Once you do this, pick out all the stories. Write them down.

Once you have all your stories written down, I want you to replace the stories with statements that start with "I am in the process of..."

The story:
"I don't have the willpower to end my fight with food."

Replace it:
"I am in the process of being able to use food for health and hunger."

The thing is, when we switch the story without using the "I am in the process" statement, our brain will automatically say, "Yeah right! You are soooooooo not even close!" However, using the progressive statement creates space for you to engage in the process of retraining your thoughts.

Once you've completed your stories and rewritten them, jump over to the Phoenix Tribe and share what you came up with.

This exercise is extremely powerful.

Once you have awareness of the stories that are no longer serving you, you have the power to shift them right away.

MANTRA

I always have the power and ability to create the life I desire.

THE BREAKING POINT
Chapter 3

The shame was seeping out of my pores. The secret was almost too painful to hide anymore. The weight of the intense pain, rage, and extreme discomfort was almost too much to handle.

I needed out of the war zone I called my mind. I needed a permanent vacation from the destructive voices in my head. I imagined what that would feel like, even just for a day, to be free from the guilt, from the pain, and from the battle. I imagined all the things I could do, think about, create, and enjoy if I wasn't fighting this battle. Life would be bliss: I would pursue my dreams, dance down the street, and fall wildly in love with life.

In the bathroom, I sat on my scale. I wasn't happy with the number on the scale when I was standing up, so I sat on it to see if I would get a different result – anything to be down another pound.

I didn't get up. I sat there with my phone in my hand looking at the review of my current diet. Beside me was a steaming cup of the shit tea. I was on cup number six at this point. I continued to read the reviews on my iPhone as I sipped my tea, feeling defeated, overwhelmed, and completely hopeless.

"Lost four pounds in two days!"

"Miracle diet! Kept the weight off for good!"

What rubbish, I thought as I thumb scrolled. It had been three days of this and I'd lost nothing, except my mind and more of my self-worth.

I obsessed over the last few days trying to figure out where I went wrong. As I stared at the screen, a text popped up from my girlfriend, Alex.

"Stroll around Clapham Common?" she asked.

"Totes, I'll be there in 20," I replied and I picked my sorry self off the floor.

I walked into my room and stood in front of the mirror. I felt disgusting, fat, and empty.

Putting on a happy face right now was going to be a struggle, but it's what I needed to do. I'd rather show up than make another excuse as to why I couldn't hang out. Besides, walking involved no calorie consumption. I was safe. I didn't need to fight food in front of other people.

I had run out of excuses as to why I couldn't eat. Excuses is a stretch — they were outright lies. Telling the closest people in my life that there were certain foods I couldn't eat for health reasons, or the time I became vegetarian because I heard it would make me skinny was eating me alive, literally.

For the first time in my life, I felt like a fake, and I wondered how I got myself so deep in this vicious cycle. People always knew me as the person who wore her heart on her sleeve at all times. In any given moment the people around me knew what I was thinking (because I had no filter), what I was feeling (because I had no shame in self-expression), and what I wanted to do because, come on, it was my way or the highway for the first 18 years of my life.

After six outfit changes, I finally grabbed my phone and texted Alex.

"I'll be right there, just getting something to eat."

More lies. I wasn't eating, I was trying to figure out what outfit doesn't make me look fat. I was 5'6" and 120 pounds soaking wet — nothing made me look fat. I could wear a Michelin man outfit and still look slim. I finally settled on an outfit, grabbed my bag, and headed out the door to meet her. We strolled around the common and chatted about boys, we talked about our dream boyfriends, what was on sale at Selfridges, and how we both drank way too much at Cafe Soll over the weekend.

I was so grateful for Alex – she was such an incredible friend. I loved everything about her. She had beautiful long curly hair and was always dressed to the nines in designer swag. As we were walking, chatting, and laughing, I remember thinking, I wish I could love myself as much as I love Alex.

I never once thought about her body, how much she weighed, or her eating habits. I just accepted her fully for who she was. I was in constant awe of her and how she treated me as a friend. For a moment, I thought to myself how I could love myself the way I loved her – I felt completely blocked – I didn't think that was possible for me. I quickly brushed the thought away, and we continued to stroll around the common.

As we chatted, Alex interrupted me mid-sentence and said, "Sam, I want to be real with you."

My heart sank and my mouth became dry. I knew where this was headed.

"I know what is going on with you, I know how much you're suffering, and I want you to know I am here to help you."

I felt equally terrified and relieved – the secret was out. I can stop pretending, stop sneaking around, and stop this battle. In that moment, I felt my whole body relax.

"You're right, I'm struggling," I admitted, which felt freeing.

After our walk, I went home, jumped in my bed, and bawled. I begged God for an answer. I begged for some kind of hunch or guidance. I needed help, I needed support, and I needed a clear indication of what I needed to do and where I needed to turn.

I covered my face with my palms and felt the tears pool in my hands and drip down my arms. I cried until my pillow was soaking wet and all my makeup was worn off.

Exhausted, I turned over onto my back, held my legs into my chest, pressed my face into my knees, and surrendered.

I would do anything to get myself out of this. I was literally crying for help –

I was sobbing for some kind of answer. The cage I had built to keep myself safe within my diet depression was strong and sturdy. From the inside, it was impossible to see my way out of it. There was no lock and key or combination, which would release me. I needed a divine intervention. This was bigger than I was.

I grew up in a Christian household, and each Sunday dad would bust into my room at 8:30 am and in his singsong voice yell at the top of his lungs,

"Up and at 'em, Sammy! Time for church!
We are leaving in 15 minutes!"

Thanks, Dad. Barely enough time to make myself look half-decent.

This same song and dance repeated every Sunday for 15 years. I would sit in church, half listening and half doodling on the paper. Sometimes, if I got lucky, my brother would play X's and O's with me so the time would pass quicker.

Growing up, I was pretty much a bible thumper. I was convinced I was going to wait until I was married to have sex and I did everything I could to ensure I was on my best behaviour for my parents, and the Church. When I was 18, this all changed. As I was entering into my diet depression, my belief in the divine was disappearing. I stopping going to church, I stopped praying, I stopped any God-related activity, and took on the world on my own. I was convinced I knew what was best for me, and I would no longer be "brainwashed" into thinking otherwise.

I knew what the energy of God felt like in my body. Call it God, the universe, the divine, my higher self – whatever the wording, I knew the feeling. I knew the feeling of totally surrendering to the belief that there was something more powerful than my human body and human mind that was constantly supporting me and having my back. I knew this part of me was still active, but it was heavily suppressed.

I lay there on my bed, and for the first time in four years, I started to pray. I yelled out for help, for guidance. I needed something to take over my body and tell me what to do.

"I give up! I fucking give up! I need you! Where are you?"
I screamed repeatedly for hours and hours.

The sun set, and I finally rolled out of bed. I walked over to my floor length mirror and just stared at myself. I talked to myself as if I was talking to God, speaking my truth and asking for what I needed. I briefly reconnected with the feeling I once felt so deeply in my body, the feeling of being supported by something outside myself. I craved that feeling again. It was clear I couldn't do this on my own.

A week later, I got off the London tube during rush hour and walked up the street to my flat. On my way upstairs, I checked the mail. There were a few white envelopes and one brown one. The brown envelopes are always boring – taxes, annoying letters, bills. I opened the door to my flat, threw my things on the floor and plonked myself on my coach in the living room. I opened the brown envelope and felt completely sick to my stomach.

"You have 30 days to leave the country."

My heart sank. I didn't want to look. I didn't want to see what it said. It's like slowing down to see a car accident: you don't really want to see it, but you keep looking.

I kept scanning the letter, and was feeling worse by the second. Luke and I, my former partner, the whole reason I moved to London, had applied for a partnership visa together so I could stay. While the visa was in progress, we had broken up, so this was the letter stating that my visa had been denied, and I needed to go back to Canada.

Naively, I assumed they wouldn't find out, and I could stay in London for another two years, which of course wasn't the case.

30 days. I needed to be gone in 30 days.

This was unbelievable – my whole life was here. I had nothing back in Canada. No job, no possessions, no home, nothing! I felt as if God himself was ripping my reality right from under my feet. I felt like I was free falling into the dark void of danger and uncertainty. I could feel my palms pool with sweat as my hands started to shake.

I double-checked the name at the top of the letter to make sure it definitely read "Samantha Skelly." It was undeniable.

I stood up and started pacing the room; my breath was shallow and quick.

I sunk into the feeling of being a victim immediately. Why me? I cried out as I started thinking about the mess I'd made for myself.

Suddenly, I remembered the sign I had asked the universe for so desperately only seven days earlier. I had begged for a sign to help me get out of this hell. I felt an ease, a feeling of calm. This was the sign I needed. I collected myself, took some deep breaths, and grounded my energy.

I closed my eyes and saw bright light, something that had never happened before. It was like a divine intervention: moments of lightness and clarity interrupted the pain I was experiencing in my body. It was as if my ego was meeting my higher self. I observed what was going on in my body as I stood there in shock.

In less than two weeks, I gave away most of my possessions and booked a one-way ticket back to Vancouver. I was leaving everything behind in London, but it was time to start fresh. It was time to find my joy again. It was finally time to put an end to my battle with food and my body.

As I sat in the airport waiting for my flight, I put on my headphones and tried to lose myself in the music. I thought about my last three years in England. I had completely lost myself. I had lost my passion, my joy, and my ambition. It was gone, and I felt flat and empty.

As the guitar chords stroked my eardrums, I allowed the tears to flow. I was releasing emotion that I had suppressed for years, and it felt freeing and terrifying at the same time. For the last few years, I had not given myself permission to feel, and allowing the feelings to flow now was overwhelming.

I continued to cry on the plane. I was so overcome by the release of emotion I had no idea why I was even crying, so I just let it happen. I'm sure the man sitting beside me was terrified.

I remember grabbing my thighs, holding my stomach, and wondering how I was going to learn to love myself. Touching my body felt foreign, as I'd been trying to run from it for so many years. I knew that learning to love myself was going to be the hardest thing I ever had to do in my whole life. I wondered what it would feel like to be at peace with food again, to feel how I felt about food when I was a child enjoying our nightly family dinners.

I wondered if there was ever going to be a time where I didn't have intense anxiety when I looked at food. I wondered if I would get to a place where I could look down at a plate of food and not be worried about how many calories it contained. I was unsure about how this was going to happen, but I trusted that because it was where I came from, it was inevitable that I would get to a place of trust with food again. I was still riddled with fear, doubt, and shame, but I couldn't go back to the hell I had created.

As I continued to sob, I wondered who I would become at the end of this journey. My ultimate fear was that I would be locked in this dark place for the rest of my life, and the idea that I would pass my patterns of disordered behaviours on to my future daughter consumed my mind. I wanted to be a mother more than anything – I want to bring life into this world; however, the thought of having a daughter while I was stuck in this cycle was terrifying.

We used to travel from Vancouver Island in British Columbia all the way to Winnipeg, Manitoba when I was a kid. Those trips were the bane of my existence. I was nicknamed "Growly" because I was angry and growled like a bear the entire road trip across Canada. Every time I didn't get my way, I would let out a massive "GRRR!" to let the rest of the family know how annoyed I was. Then, dad would pop in some Tony Robbins to try to pacify me. Tony's music about leverage and needing a reason to change your life really spoke to me.

As the plane taxied to the runway, I started to think of leverage. What was it costing me to stay stuck in this place, hating my body, fighting with food and having my mind race every moment of every day wondering how many calories were going to be in my next meal? I wondered how I was going to raise children, build a business, and be fully invested in my partner when I was so heavily stuck in the shit storm I created.

The realization that I had potentially cost myself a lifetime of contentment slapped me in the face and left a lingering sting. It was the first time I felt the visceral pain of my decisions, a zoomed out look at the mess I had created.

As the plane was taking off, I visualized leaving my pain on the tarmac – leaving the stress, anxiety, disordered eating, and hatred on the ground waiting to be run over by another plane. I was over it. I was so done with hiding, and my radiant soul was begging to be released.

My beautiful, effervescent soul was so heavily suppressed by my fear, and she wanted out. I could hear her speaking to me with love, and I had silenced her with hate. Day after day I dulled her shine and stuffed her deeper and deeper into a dark hole.

As we floated above England tilting left to right and right to left, I felt a wave of ease overcome my body, as just the mere visualization of ending this battle with food and my body felt blissful. I was determined. I was going to do whatever it took to end this battle and get back to the real me again. I knew she was down there somewhere, and it was time to find her again.

PRACTICE IN ACTION

You're allowed to let go. You're allowed to create a new reality. When that plane took off from the tarmac in London, I promised myself I was going to let go of everything that wasn't serving me anymore, and I can assure you, my list was about a mile long. So many things in my life were an energetic drain on my soul. If I was as committed as I said I was, I needed to release these things from my life. May that be people, clothes, scales, behaviours, beliefs, whatever — it was time to let go and become the highest, best, and most authentic version of myself.

I had to take a closer look at all the areas of my life.

I asked myself the question, "What do I need to let go of in order to become the highest, best, and most authentic version of me?"

EXERCISE #3

I want you to make a list of what you need to let go. The first step is simply getting clear with what that is, and then it's a process of releasing.

When you have your list complete, spend some time with it. Hold it in your hands and read it over. It's time to release all that is not serving you at the highest level.

Light some candles, rub your lavender essential oil on both wrists and on your heart, grab a bowl, crumple your letter into the bowl, and light the edges of the paper. Watch the paper disintegrate while you repeat, "It's safe to let go. I deserve to let go" silently to yourself. Feel the lightness and space that comes with this exercise. You are clearing space on your energetic landscape to make space for the new.

You've got this.

Set aside two hours, make a cup of tea, grab a blanket, and cuddle up somewhere warm. Do this exercise with compassion and love. Be kind to yourself.

MANTRA

I am safe to let go. I deserve to let go.

THE STRUGGLE IS NOT REAL
Chapter 4

I spent the entire day Googling and drinking coffee and looking for answers to end my battle with food. I am quite certain I read every single article or video containing the following keywords and phrases:

How to eat like a normal person
How to stop being crazy around food
How to stop using food as a drug
How to love your body
How to sort your life out
How to get out of your own shit storm
How to stop sucking at life

After weeks of researching, reading, and watching a ridiculous number of YouTube videos, I got absolutely nowhere. I felt defeated, alone, and broken. I was so overwhelmed by all the non-sense on the internet. If one more of these full make-up-faced pretty girls on YouTube told me to "slow down" when I eat or "meditate" to make myself present, I was going to punch my computer screen. Each day, I got more and more angry, and each day I felt more and more defeated.

No one fucking understands me.

Eating mindfully is not really going to help me sort my life out.

While breathing and slowing down while eating seemed like a great idea, it just didn't work for me. I tried and failed and tried again – funny how every damn blog suggests this idea. The problem with food is so much deeper than that.

I just wanted to throw the food across the kitchen and scream. There must be something I am missing here, some trick I'm not getting.

I read the reviews of some of these suggestions – women speaking of their triumphs and how they had overcome binge eating for good.

What annoyed me the most was the fact that I am pretty damn clever. I am quite certain that I can figure out and master whatever I put my mind to. I've done this repeatedly with various things in my life, but when it came to just using food for health and hunger, I was totally clueless.

Every night when I went to bed, my brain was completely exhausted from spinning with confusion and frustration. The ease and lightness I felt when the plane left London was slowly dissipating, and I was beginning to think this was just my destiny; this was just something I had to live with for the rest of my life. It felt like a terminal illness that I didn't have the power to overcome.

Being the headstrong, stubborn woman that I was (and still am), I told myself I was going to do this on my own. I was going to figure it out and push through without telling anyone how much this struggle had a hold on me. After all, this was my hidden secret that I kept from the world. I wanted to struggle in silence and heal in silence. This plan made sense to me. Alex knew, because I simply couldn't lie to her when she asked me about it, but other than that, I pushed through pretending I was all-good. I needed to be strong for the rest of the world, because I was the one everyone went to for advice and support. There was no way I could let on that I was weak and struggling. My ego simply couldn't handle that kind of damage.

Rather than getting the help I needed, I pushed through, month after month after month. I read and reread every article and blog I could find to ensure I didn't miss something. I threw money at programs that promised the world and severely under delivered. Seeing my bank account drain at the same rate as my self-worth made my skin crawl.

I sat on the balcony of my Vancouver apartment and cried. It had been months of banging my head against the wall trying to figure this out. Tears streamed down my face, and my body sank to the ground. I cried on that 18th floor balcony until I couldn't cry anymore. Every ounce of mascara was gone, my t-shirt was soaked, and I didn't care how many people in the streets below had heard me ugly cry.

All I could hear in my mind were the words, GO GET HELP. I had no idea where they came from – the ethers of the universe? Perhaps. However, I didn't question it – I just followed it. After months of hitting resistance, coming up against fear, and doubting the fact I would ever be normal again, I got over myself and decided to hit up Google again, this time for another reason.

I typed "Life Coach Vancouver" into the search box.

I hate the term life coach. What does that even mean? How can you be a coach of life itself? To me it sounded like a rather grandiose concept. Regardless, I Googled and scrolled until I found someone who resonated with me.

Ray was a grey haired man with wise eyes and about 60 years old. I saved his details, but I didn't have it in me to contact him just yet. A few days later, I attended a personal development seminar in another fruitless attempt at searching externally to fix my internal problem.

While I was there, I sat next to a beautiful girl with blonde hair named Mackenzie, and we spoke about what we do in the world. I didn't tell her I was just a lost soul looking for my feet again. She told me she was a business coach operating in Vancouver and New York, and she immediately inspired me. Later in the conversation, she told me she was coached by a man in Vancouver whom she described as incredible. After a little bit of digging, I realized that her coach was Ray, the grey haired, wise eyed man I Googled just a few days before. Ok, this was a sign. I needed to reach out to Ray.

Within a few hours of sending my first email, he responded.

Oh god, I thought, this is actually happening. I could feel his calming and gentle voice though the text in the email. I felt good – I felt accomplished. You know that feeling when you buy a book? You don't even have to read it and you already feel like a better, more educated human. I already felt like I was in the right place with Ray.

When I met him for coffee for the first time, it felt like the first day of school or a new job, and I was equally terrified and excited. The human version of Ray was the same as the online version. He greeted me with such grace and love, that it felt like a warm hug of safe masculine energy. I immediately loved Ray, and over the next two hours, I hung on his every word and listened carefully. He spoke of his lovely wife, his family, and the work he does in the world. I left the meeting feeling hope for the first time in a long time, as he was able to already identify some of the stories I was telling myself that kept me feeling stuck in the vicious cycle with food and my body, which, to my surprise had absolutely nothing to do with food. Go figure.

I went home and emailed Ray right away. I told him how much I appreciated his time, and told him I definitely wanted to work with him. I was so proud of myself for taking such massive steps in the right direction. For a long time, four years to be exact, I took action in the opposite direction, miles away from my higher self. I was proud of myself for the first time in a long time, and not the kind of proud I felt after meeting my calorie intake for the day. This was different: a deep soul level kind of proud.

At my first session with Ray, I knew I was in good company. He lived and worked in the penthouse of a gorgeous downtown Vancouver building that reminded me of a posh hotel. When I arrived, orchids, my favorite flower, welcomed me, and the pleasant smell of the room and panoramic view of the mountains put me at ease. Ray brewed us some coffee, and we sat on his plush leather couches and started chatting. Ray asked me general questions to get to know me, and then the real question came.

"So, what is it that you need help with?"

In that moment, I felt the pain of the last four years begin to pour out of my eyes. I ugly cried and couldn't get a word out. As soon as I tried to speak, I would choke on my tears, trying to catch my breath so I could simply just cry harder. I couldn't remember the last time I gave myself permission to just break down and let myself unleash the emotion I was feeling in front of another human being. Even when Alex first told me she knew what was going on, I held back until I was in the safety of my flat before I let the tears flow.

Ray just looked at me, holding space for me as I released four years of pain from my body. I felt liberated, while at the same time feeling resistant to allowing myself to breakdown. I was going against my identity of "having it all together." I let myself be ok with it – I was safe – this is why I came to see Ray.

After what felt like a lifetime of me releasing all this emotion, I could finally catch my breath long enough to speak.

"I just can't do this anymore, Ray. I need help."

Admitting I needed help to another human made me feel as vulnerable as I would be walking around downtown with no clothes on. I was officially at the depths of my battle, relying on the support of another human to guide me through the muddy disaster I had gotten myself into.

There was a silence after I spoke. Ray looked at me with his piercing eyes and nodded. The silence continued, but I looked away. I was in such a vulnerable place – I felt exposed. I opened my journal, grabbed my pen and wrote on the first page. Everything changes now. I dated the page. I was not going back. I was ruthlessly committed to my transformation, and I would do anything it takes to get back to who I once was, and it all started now.

Ray explained to me that this was going to be a process. We were no longer going to put a Band-Aid on a bullet wound, and we were going to get into the depths of my soul and heal the wounds that had been created in my body. It was finally time to heal from the inside out: there was no diet in the world that would be able to heal my emotional field.

When he first explained all this, I was highly triggered. Firstly, I have the patience of a toddler. I want everything yesterday. Secondly, I was terrified of what I might find if I looked beyond my surface level emotions.

"What if I can't handle what comes up when I explore my body?" I asked Ray, with fear in my voice and terror in my face.

Ray assured me that my body wouldn't give me anything I couldn't handle, that we were in a safe container to grow, heal and transform together. All of these hippy dippy words were throwing me off a little. "Holding space... safe container." I literally had no idea what those phrases even meant.

I just kept nodding, throwing all my trust in a man I met on the internet. In the dating world, that would have been ridiculous, but this felt fine. I needed to have blind faith. I couldn't see the next step. I couldn't see ANY steps. I was blind to the process, and all I knew was that the pain of my struggle was more painful than the uncertainty I felt. The next step was right in front of me. I didn't know what it was or how it was going to feel but I knew it was there.

I remembered when I was younger, and mom would yell at me to shut off all the lights downstairs before I went to bed. The light switch was on one side of the room and I had to walk to the other side of the room to make my way upstairs. After I shut off the lights, it was pitch black. I felt completely blind in the darkness. I had to feel my way to the foot of the staircase and then take the first step, hoping I got it right.

This process was like climbing the stairs in the dark. I knew the staircase was there, I just needed to take a step and not be afraid of failing. This tested my desire to be perfect at everything. I was such a perfectionist; I even tried to be perfect at trying to be perfect. In a competition of who was the biggest perfectionist, I'd win first place and hold my trophy above my head with pride. Except the trophy was incredibly heavy and weighing me down in every aspect of my life.

So often, we think we need to see the entire staircase in order to take the first step. This is not how life works, and it never will work this way. Life rewards those who take action without having a 100% guarantee in place. One of my mentors, Philip McKernan, always says, "In the absence of clarity, take action." This is one of the simplest, yet profoundly life-changing ideas we can adopt. Blind faith is required to progress. Progress creates happiness, even if it's the "wrong" choice. And let's be clear, it's only your mind that is labelling the choice as wrong. In fact, it's always the right choice, and everything is working out for you in perfect timing. We usually label situations the wrong choice if it feels heavy, we have conflict, or it creates pain. This, too, has been divinely orchestrated in your life. The pain is there for you to learn from it. The pain is there for you to get curious about it and ask yourself questions, which will aid in your healing.

The pain in my body was so severe that I suppressed it and ignored it. Finding ways to numb the pain was something I took on as a hobby, of course food was the most obvious choice, but it didn't stop there. I had a laundry list of distractions I could do in order to ignore the pain that was bubbling deep within my soul. I used to find any excuse in the world not to clean the bathroom when I was a child. I would beg and plead with my mom to make my chores not include bathroom duty, and now, I willingly clean the bathroom to avoid feeling the pain in my body. My, how times have changed.

It's important to release the need to know the outcomes of our actions before we actually do something. Emotional healing and growth isn't linear. One plus two does not equal three when we are working on our emotional field. This tested every truth I had about how the world works and frustrated me to my core, until I decided to surrender to the process and allow something bigger than myself take over. Relinquishing control and allowing the process to unfold exactly how it was meant to unfold was something I wish I had grasped early in my recovery process. I probably would have dramatically decreased the time I spent trying to figure it out on my own.

In a world that values logic over intuition, we need to believe in the force outside of ourselves in order to give ourselves full permission to heal and grow. As beautiful, sharp, and clever your mind is, it's not going to do you any favours in healing the battle you have with food and your body.

You must feel in order to heal.

The majority of the women I work with are incredibly intelligent woman, highly aware of the pain they are in without a clue about how to get rid of it. They've told me that they've tried everything and nothing works. It's not because they don't have the intelligence or the willpower to heal, rather, they are just going about it the wrong way, as I was. I was trying to think my way out of my disorder, which just perpetuated the disorder even more.

You are divinely supported in your healing journey. You weren't designed to suffer; you were designed for happiness and ease. When you make a decisive decision, you're not going to suffer, and if you take blind faith in the direction that is most conducive to the highest, best, and most authentic version of yourself, you will be graciously rewarded. You have the power and ability to move through any resistance you meet on the path of liberation. The universe has your back.

PRACTICE IN ACTION

I believe one of the main reasons why I chose to stay stuck for so long was because I wasn't aware how much it was costing me to stay stuck in the battle with food and my body. I drastically lowered my standards to fit with the pain I was dealing with. There was a time where I just settled on having a mediocre life. I settled with knowing that I was just going to deal with this issue.

When Ray and I met, he asked me a question that literally changed my life: "What is it costing you to stay stuck?" I'm not talking about finances, although, money does come into play, as you will see in later chapters, but there were massive costs to my wellbeing to stay stuck in my personal hell.

We discussed the difference between where I was and where I wanted to be. I saw the difference, and it was massive. There was a great discrepancy between who I was being and who I was projecting on Instagram. This felt awful, because the image of myself I projected wasn't real. I felt like fraud.

EXERCISE #4

I want you to think of all the things that are suffering because you remain stuck in the battle with food and your body.

What is it costing you to...
...wake up every morning hating your body?
...constantly fight food?
...feel stuck and uncomfortable in your life?
...say no to social interactions?
...hide your secret from loved ones?

Once you clearly identify what it is costing you, then I want you to create a list of things you would have access to or be able to do if you cleared up all of that mental energy you spend obsessing over food and your body.

"I would finally start writing."
"I would be more present with my children."
"I'd be having way more sex with my partner."
"I'd finally go on holiday and wear that black bikini."

Whatever it is for you, get super clear of what it's costing you, and then what you will have access to once you end the fight. When you've completed the exercise, jump on over to the Phoenix Tribe and share with us.

MANTRA

I fully deserve to attract all I desire into my life.

THE DARK SIDE OF PERFECTIONISM
Chapter 5

I erased the two lines I wrote down, smacked my head on the table, and let out a sigh. My green tea was cold, and it was 6:33 pm. Two hours after I started to write.

Nothing made sense.

Everything I wrote was stupid or I assumed nobody would even care. So, I sat there, with my palms in my face and a pit in my stomach. I knew I needed to get the words out, because I was on a deadline - it couldn't be late. That was unacceptable.

I kept going and going and going, until I finally erased the entire article, slammed my screen down, dumped out my six-hour-old green tea, and went to bed. I lay in bed thinking about how much time I just wasted trying to get a few words out on paper. My mind was racing thinking of all the things I should have done today, could have done, or could have done better. Delivering a line better in an audition, hitting that triple turn with more grace, or getting that stupid question correct on a math exam: nothing was ever good enough. When I thought I did ok, I would set the bar even higher, never able to celebrate my accomplishments or feel good about myself.

Being in the performance industry only strengthened and reinforced my commitment to perfectionism. Rejection is just how I experienced life. It was all I really knew. When I did have a miracle or a victory in school or in my career, I would quickly sabotage myself by creating a new goal and not appreciating the accomplishment of the current one. The soundtrack of my mind was a constant tune of "not good enough."

Compliments slid off my back like water, and when someone would take the time to compliment my work, or me, I would think they were mildly delusional. How could anything that I did be worth praise? I never registered words of praise; I just awkwardly laughed them off hoping someone would change the subject. This pattern went on for years, but in some way, it served me by allowing me to excel in most areas of my life. However, the darkness and pain that came with the success just wasn't worth the excellence it delivered.

Living as a perfectionist means thinking and living in "black and white" – there are no grey areas. You are either perfect with your diet, or you throw in the towel and completely screw it up, all while shaming yourself. Perfectionism is the death of happiness. It's impossible to feel happy and at peace with yourself when you are on a constant path of self-sabotage.

Comparison and perfectionism are the thieves of joy – when we are comparing and distancing ourselves from "the goal," we aren't being present and appreciating all we have in the present moment. Goals, especially weight goals, are manufactured in the mind – they are pre-decided without any consultation from the body, the soul, or the spirit.

I can't even remember how old I was when I started to believe that I wasn't good enough unless I was perfect. I had a best friend growing up: Carly. She was tall, beautiful, and an actor, as well as a singer. All the boys loved Carly - she was always dating a boy three or four years older than her (when you're twelve, this is a BIG deal) and was adored by the other students and the teachers. Because Carly and I were the closest of friends, I always felt like I was living in her shadow. I always felt like she was the singer and I was just the awkward backup dancer. I always wanted to be like Carly. I wanted to dress like her, look like her, wear the same makeup as her, and date the older boys as she did. I was on a constant quest to level up to where she was. I wasn't my own person during these times. I would bow down to her and do everything in my power to make Carly happy, because God forbid she would ditch me as a friend. We did everything she wanted to do, and I went along with it, not making a fuss and just being okay with it. Carly was my benchmark of perfection, because even at twelve years old, I was obsessed with my appearance, my grades in school, and my performances.

This was the start of it all – the catalyst to a decade of living as a perfectionist. It's really easy to hate your body and in turn develop disordered eating when everything has to be perfect. When I no longer had my dancing career as an outlet to channel my perfectionism, it manifested in my relationship with food and my body. I had an idea of what perfect was, based on magazine front covers and commercial ads, and if I felt I wasn't hitting that benchmark, I would force myself to undergo a restrictive diet until I felt on-par with the ridiculous standards I had set in place for myself. My body was the enemy during this time, and because I was never satisfied with my body, food became my obsession because it was something I could control.

Disordered eating patterns are a result of poor body image - there is no reason to be obsessive over food if you're happy with the relationship you have with your body. My perfectionism found its way into managing my caloric deficiency. Perfectionism found peace within the obsession, the constant nagging, the overplayed rhythm of "not enough," the number counting, and the shaming.

Perfectionism is run by the ego and the mind. The body already knows it's perfect the way it is. The ever-powerful mind tries to waver this belief. The mind is what creates that black and white thinking, that all or nothing mentality. Either you are following the diet exactly to plan, or you throw in the towel and binge on everything in the house, and then some.

In the thick of my battle, my perfectionism was at an all-time high. I genuinely thought I could "shame myself skinny." I was convinced that the harder I was on myself, the quicker I was going to get to my "ideal" weight. I just needed to force harder, restrict more, and be an even bigger raging bitch to myself. I couldn't let go of the hate, because if I did, I would spin into a frenzy, devouring everything in sight and blowing up to 300 pounds. In the mind of a perfectionist, we justify these behaviours by convincing ourselves and the world perfectionism is the road to success. In the thick of it, we are convinced it's healthy behaviour to bring the hammer down on ourselves day after day. When in reality, perfectionism is a shield. It's a heavy price to pay to hide from the world. We refuse to admit we are human, we refuse the fact we are flawed and beautiful, as according to a perfectionist, it's either one or the other. The two cannot co-exist. Perfectionists assume this shield will protect them, when in reality it's the very thing keeping them stuck in the madness.

Perfectionism is not synonymous with self-improvement. Perfectionism, at the very core, is a desperate cry to gain the approval and acceptance of those around us. We fear at our core that we are fundamentally broken; we fear we aren't good enough. So often, our perfectionist tendencies are easily justified by using the term "health." I see it all the time, "But, it's for health reasons!" I can sniff that excuse out a mile away, and I used it repeatedly. Every diet I tried was masked as a "health kick," when really it was another desperate attempt to drop the last five pounds I was desperate to strip from my body. The underlying core belief of taking action for health reasons would be, "How can I improve?" whereas, the perfectionist takes action because there is a core fear of "What will they think?" This is the difference between taking action from a place of fear and taking action from a place of love. It's a massive difference.

When we have our minds set on an intention, and we start from a place of pure love and self-acceptance, the journey of getting there is much more pleasant. We see transformation, and it's sustainable, because we aren't killing ourselves to get there. We must start from a place of total body acceptance and love, having a clear intention of how we want to feel. For most people, this is the hardest thing to do. They are terrified that if they decide to love themselves, just for a moment, they are going to gain weight. If they no longer hate their bodies, they won't be in a state of heavy restriction, and this halting fear stops many people from freeing themselves from the diet-binge cycle.

The fundamental reason why the weight loss industry is a billion dollar business is simply that they play on peoples' insecurities and false hopes. They know that the vast majority of women hate their bodies, and weight loss companies use this knowledge to their advantage. As long as we hate ourselves, we will continue to throw money at the system, hoping for a different result. We are convinced that we've not tried it all yet, so we continue the search – the next miracle pill, the next cleanse, the next trend that will be the golden ticket to have them dancing around like the women in the tampon commercials.

We live in a world of instant gratification. We are conditioned to think we don't need to do any of the hard work; we are conditioned to think that we can put another bandage on a bullet wound. Perfectionists are victims to this kind of marketing and debauchery.

Perfectionism embodies the notion and deep belief that our worth is outside of who we are at the core, as if the light and power that is innate within us is dismissed, and our worth is all dependent on what we do, what we accomplish, and how well we accomplish it. This externalization of self-worth means your self-worth is always on the line. Failure to recognize the worth within propels perfectionists into a quest of searching outside of who they are, latching onto labels and identities and finding significance in things outside of who they are. It's a never-ending battle, because there will always be a new benchmark to reach when we don't recognize the brilliance within who we are at the core. Perfectionism is addictive, because when we invariably do experience shame, judgment, and blame, we often believe it's because we weren't perfect enough. So, rather than questioning the faulty logic of perfectionism, we become even more entrenched in our quest to live, look, and do everything just right.

Because as perfectionists we are hypercritical of ourselves, by default, we become extremely critical of others. When we are body shaming to death, we also are doing it to others. We compare, measure up, and create unrealistic standards for others, just as we do for ourselves. We are quick to see ourselves as better or worse than others. This creates a lack of intimacy and connection with those who mean the most to us. Energetically we are distancing ourselves from them, because we fear they will see the broken parts of us, so we are careful to keep them at arm's length.

I grew up in a family where I was heavily praised for my accomplishments. I have the most loving and supportive family, and I was constantly striving to please them and to show them I was doing a good job. I showed this through striving to get good grades, excelling in dance, booking acting gigs, and being a minimalist. In my eyes, accomplishments were synonymous with love and acceptance. This pattern was learned, it wasn't taught. Children crave love from those around them, namely their parental figures. Love wasn't limited in my family. We were abundant in love; however, I felt being just me wasn't quite good enough. I needed to do more, be more, accomplish more. These beliefs presented themselves as a constant need for acceptance and approval as a child, and then spun into severe disordered eating patterns as an adult.

To escape the tyranny of perfectionism, you have to be okay with what is, be present, and in full acceptance of where you're at, with a deep profound knowing that no matter how hard you are on yourself, it won't propel you into the promised land that you have so carefully crafted in your mind.

No amount of body shaming will allow you to experience the emotions of lightness, ease, and peace in your body. Transcending this hate into gratitude will allow you to see the good within what is.

Shifting from the perfectionist mindset of "all or nothing" into a state of "loving what is" was one of the most profound journeys of my life. When I was able to settle into my body and feel my emotions with no desire to change anything or prove anything to anyone, I felt a deep sense of peace and liberation, one that had been missing from my body for years. I now have a tattoo that says, "Loving what is," which reminds me, even when I am in the thick of the mess, it's all a blessing and a lesson. Everything is happening for me, not to me. Shifting my perception of pain now allows me to look for the blessings in all things, and this is the best gift I could have ever given myself.

It's time to take off your badge of perfectionism – it's time to get messy and allow the pain of your mistakes to be the catalyst for your own healing and growth. If not, you will stay stuck and stagnant in your safe box of perfectionism. It's time to give yourself permission to make mistakes. You're human – start acting like one.

PRACTICE IN ACTION

It's time to break the pattern of perfectionism. It only leads to procrastination, self-sabotage, people pleasing, and just being a total control freak. When things need to be perfect we aim to control our surrounding to suit the image of how things should be that we have in our minds.

A perfectionist is always on edge, always on guard, and feels the weight of the world on her shoulders; therefore, the weight tends to end up on her body. A perfectionist is hyper critical of themselves; therefore, they are hyper critical of the world. Always judging, measuring up, and comparing, this keeps the perfectionist in a constant state of competition and negativity. You're holding onto something, and when you grip on, you are not only holding on emotionally, but you hold on physically as well. Weight represents what we are holding onto. Weight can represent a difficult conversation we are too scared to have, a story we feel shame about that needs to be healed, or a habit that is causing us emotional pain. Through this process, we are releasing all that isn't serving us emotionally, and the body will respond in the most natural way possible. Weight loss is never the goal; however, it's often the result.

EXERCISE #5

In this exercise, I want you to look at your life and figure out all the areas you're controlling. Let's be real, it's not just the food you're trying to control; your need for control is percolating in every area of your life. Look at the areas in your life that you view in black and white. Perfectionists have a hard time playing in the grey area. Once you find out what areas you're trying to hyper control, I want you to ask yourself, "If I were to let go of control in this area, what is the worst that could happen?"

We cling on for control because we don't trust ourselves to make the right decision. We fear we won't be able to handle the outcome, so we hold on to the hope that things won't change too much. Take time with this, think of all the areas in your life that this is affecting. Once you're done, pop on over to the Phoenix Tribe and share your findings.

MANTRA

Everything is working out for me and coming to me in divine timing.

SILENCED BY SCARCITY
Chapter 6

I find it fascinating our society is so rooted in and committed to scarcity when we live in such a beautifully abundant world. We live in a world where we quite literally have access to whatever we want, in copious amounts. Each of us has the birthright to attract as much abundance into our life as we desire. We all have handshake agreements with the universe that we will live our best lives, and this includes being able to live without lack and limitation. It's a common belief that we don't deserve abundance – we don't deserve all the money, love, and freedom this world has to offer, so we limit ourselves. We make excuses as to why we don't need something or can't obtain it. We have conditioned ourselves for scarcity in an overly abundant world.

You likely learned the programs that are running your behaviours at a very young age. These programs were forced on you and because you didn't yet have the wisdom or experience to think or believe otherwise, you've taken these programs on and have been reinforcing them for years. The most important thing to note here is that you do not own those programs. They are just unconsciously running in the background, interrupting the flow of abundance to you. The majority of people are completely unaware of the fact scarcity programs are manifesting and growing on their emotional field. Awareness brings clarity to these programs, and with enough clarity and grit, we can begin the process of transcending these patterns into higher state of consciousness and of course, abundance.

Scarcity is ingrained and blueprinted in us to force us to take immediate action. The idea of "getting our share" is strong; therefore, we are compelled to want the things in our lives that we think will be taken away from us.

The very thing we think we have to have is probably not even the best thing for us, but we simply don't want to be without it. Scarcity surrounds most things in life.

There's not enough money.
There's not enough time.
There aren't enough men/women.
There aren't enough jobs.
There's not enough freedom.
And so on.

Our relationship to scarcity is not localized to one area: it percolates and transcends into all areas of our lives; therefore, if we want to address one area we must look at the larger picture. "How you do anything is how you do everything" embodies the fact that the programs we have innate within us are practised out in all areas of our lives. If we have severe money scarcity, this will also be evident in our relationship to food.

When it comes to our relationship with food, scarcity is the driving force to keeping us stuck in a state of binge eating. Scarcity is a powerful force, which propels us into a binge where we consume everything in sight. The majority of people who struggle with binge eating don't understand these behaviours are being driven by a subconscious belief that isn't even their own.

Humans adapt beliefs that we inherit. The beliefs start as a story, then we to go work finding evidence to support these stories, and then they turn into gospel in our minds. Most of the time these beliefs are operating in the background of our minds, and we don't know we are running a program that isn't serving our self. When we don't have awareness around the beliefs and programs we are running, there is no space to shift them. We can only begin to shift and transcend these beliefs when we are aware of them and we realize what the beliefs are costing us.

Claire joined me on one of my retreats in Whistler. Claire had suffered with binge eating for the majority of her life. When we first met each other, I was amazed at her level of confidence. She came into the room shining like a light, sat down, and began interacting with the other women immediately. Often it takes a few days for the women to all connect with each other, but Claire jumped right in and held nothing back; it was a refreshing and beautiful first impression.

During our first group session, Claire shared her story – her painful story of literally having to lock herself out of her house so she wouldn't eat everything in sight.

I asked her immediately, "Claire, what is your relationship like to money?"

She sighed and shot me an evil look. "What the hell does this have to do with food?" she said with haste.

"Everything," I repeated.

I could see her frustration and unease overwhelm her. She started panting, her chest was inflamed, and I saw her reaching for the tissues, which were on the table in front of her. Claire was uncomfortable, and I could feel her pain as the circle was silent waiting for her to answer or for me to say something to break the awkward silence. I could feel the silence not only triggering Claire, but also the other women as they related Claire's experience to their own lives.

"Claire, you are living your entire life from a place of scarcity and fear. It's not about the food. The issue is much deeper."

She finally made eye contact with me, and I noticed the tears running down her face. I could literally see the pain trickle down her skin as every nerve in her body was fully activated. I was fully certain I had hit a nerve within Claire, one that was lying just below the surface and she hadn't been aware of until now. I had lovingly stuck my needle right where it hurt. Claire's entire demeanor changed: truth bombs can hurt, and they can lead to a tremendous amount of healing.

Scarcity was keeping Claire stuck in the diet and binge cycle. It was the one thing that was leading her into chaotic episodes of binging several times a week. When we have scarcity around food, we believe that if we don't eat everything in sight immediately, we simply won't have access to it in the future. We don't trust that we will be provided for, so we stock up for future.

This is a classic feast or famine scenario. We need to remember: this is how we were designed from day one, but it's not a truth we hold today.

Dieting puts our bodies into a severe state of deprivation to inflict weight loss in an attempt to change our bodies. Dieting is a short term Band-Aid on a bullet wound approach. What we are really searching for is feeling, but we are too caught up in the mechanics of calorie restriction to achieve that feeling. Because dieting is not sustainable, we eventually give up on our 1000-calorie-a-day diet fads and return to our old ways of overeating. This is where this combination gets dangerous. Binge eating is a natural physical reaction to deprivation. Retreating from binge eating right after a diet is one of the hardest things to do. We are conditioned, by nature, for feast and famine; therefore, when we stop a diet we immediately go into feast mode, wanting to eat everything in sight. Our body is terrified that we are going to experience a famine again soon, so we take advantage of the food we have access to in the moment.

This no longer becomes a conversation about having will power. We can't out power our bodies — they always win the fight against our minds.

Having a predetermined scarcity mindset and restricting calories is a disastrous combination. It's a battle you simply can't win. There is so much frustration in this, because people aren't aware either is taking place in their bodies. They aren't aware that their scarcity mindset paired with restrictive behaviours is nearly an impossible battle to break free from without awareness.

When I pointed out to Claire that her entire life was run by her scarcity mindset, she was able to make sense of her behaviour. For her entire life, she was trying to change her diet to stop her binge eating behaviours, which only perpetuated the issue.

I called Claire a year after the retreat where she had adapted an inner belief of abundance. I could tell from when she picked up the phone that there had been a shift. She explained to me how her commitment to abundance had not only ended her binge episodes, but she was now releasing weight from a place of love rather than being stuck in the endless diet/binge cycle. Claire had said to me at the retreat, with fear in her eyes and tears running down her face, "I just want to eat like a normal person," and at the end of the call, I asked her, "So tell me Claire, are you finally eating like a normal person?" Claire laughed hysterically and told me how she never knew this could be possible for her.

This is a classic example of how unconscious beliefs can run our lives and determine the quality of our lives if we let them. Claire's belief was, "There isn't enough for me," which wove its way into her thoughts, feelings, actions, and results. Claire is now living in a beautiful state of abundance and is grateful she decided to confront those beliefs head on.

Desire becomes addiction when we are operating from a scarcity mindset. We have a craving for something to "take the edge off" or "soothe the soul." However, that desire comes from being hungry for an emotion, not ice cream. Desire, when fulfilled in a safe, abundant way, can be one of the most self-gratifying acts of self-love. When we know we are craving expression, sexual play, fun, or connection, and we allow ourselves to experience that feeling with full awareness from a place of love, we give ourselves permission to love and be loved. It's a beautiful exchange.

When our innate desire for emotional fulfillment is met through an external quick fix, we are always left in a state of searching. When we bypass what we are actually hungry for and dive in for the ice cream, we aren't honouring our true desires and are therefore breaking agreements with ourselves. This paradigm, paired with a pre-existing scarcity mindset, is a recipe for disaster and a hypnotic binge-eating episode. This is when we simply can't stop putting the spoon to our mouths in an attempt to fill the void we feel in our bodies. This void will never be fulfilled with food. No amount of ice cream can fill an emotional void.

When Claire was sharing her story with me at the retreat she said to me, "I just don't understand, I can eat everything in my house and still not be totally satisfied." This is a prime example of artificially meeting desire with a mindset of scarcity. When we think it's the last tub of Ben and Jerry's ice cream on the planet, we will do everything it takes to make sure we demolish it. When we are operating from a scarcity mindset, we are all up in our heads, and we're completely disconnected from our bodies. It's not our bodies that want the ice cream. It's our minds. Our minds think the ice cream will compensate for our lack of feeling. But it won't, and this is why we overeat.

Which is why the concept of body shaming really makes no sense. How we can hate our bodies when they are simply the product of decisions we've made in our minds? When we change our minds, we change our bodies. When we dig into the programs, beliefs, and patterns that are running us, we are able to access clarity, ease, and freedom.

And this is how we change the game.

In order to shift the chaotic energy that has the potential to take over our lives, we must approach it from a deep, core level. It's not enough to just stop eating that much or count calories to ensure we don't overeat. It is essential that we begin to adopt a mindset of abundance if we want to win the fight with food. At a fundamental level, we need to rewire our commitment to scarcity. A mindset of scarcity has been created for the majority of our lives, it's simply rooted in who we are when we are born, and our society reinforces this belief. It's completely counter-intuitive to the flow of the universe, but as humans, we can't quite grasp the concept of unlimited abundance, so it's safer to believe in what we know logically. Using affirmations and changing our beliefs allows us to welcome in the idea of abundance:

I will always have everything I need.
I attract wealth in unlimited quantities.
I will always have enough food to fuel my body.
The universe always provides for me.

When we begin to say these affirmations, they will challenge our current belief system. A small part of us will want to keep rooted in our old beliefs and will do everything in its power to call bullshit on these beliefs. You have be ok with this, as it is completely normal in the rewiring process. We are simply putting a part of our ego to death, and that can feel like free falling. Even though we know our scarcity mindset is not serving us at the highest level, it's comfortable because it's something we know. Giving ourselves permission to adapt to these new beliefs is not only noble and courageous, but the highest act of self-love. When we declare to the universe we are going to start living in alignment with the flow of abundance, rather than going against it, we begin to create channels of miracles to reach us more effectively.

Scarcity blocks miracles from entering our lives. The universe is abundant in miracles, waiting to be showered onto those who are fully ready to not only accept them, but also notice and appreciate them. Miracles from the divine are in complete alignment with how the universe operates and how we were designed to live. It's a shame we operate in such states of scarcity when we have access to unlimited abundance. Our higher selves are waiting patiently for us to surrender fully to their power, to guide us and heal us.

As soon as we can welcome the idea of abundance and we believe we deserve it and experience it, we will see it start to manifest.

At this point, you might be thinking,
"Yeah, right, Sam. I'll believe it when I see it."

This statement is rooted in scarcity – it doubts the magic and miracles that are abundant and ready to be given to us. We need to switch this belief to "when I believe it, I will see it". When we can attune our minds and our inner energies to an abundant state, we will start to see abundance manifesting in our lives. This is a universal law. However, our doubt intervenes and often doesn't allow us to experience the feeling of abundance before we have it. This is where the majority of the world is blocked; they don't allow themselves to feel abundant until they see the numbers in their bank account.

When I was first growing my company, I was struggling to adapt an abundance mindset in terms of money. I was terrified I was going to lose all my money and not be able to bring my mission to life. I would worry about all my clients suddenly dropping off and not being able to serve and survive any longer. There was no way this was ever going to happen. I knew what I was offering the world was so needed and my clients were having incredible breakthroughs on a daily basis. But, I allowed my scarcity mindset to be activated for a while, which brought forth a lot of fear. I allowed my mind to go back to default, welcoming in the old programs of scarcity into my experience.

Without paying careful attention to them, these programs have a tendency to reintegrate themselves back into our lives if we aren't aware of what we are allowing ourselves to think. I spent the majority of my life in a state of scarcity, which was a huge factor in developing my disordered eating patterns. While I spent three years overcoming my eating disorder, I spent a lot of time reprogramming my scarcity mindset, because I knew it had an incredible amount of leverage on me. When I felt the liberation from living in abundance, I stopped being so aware of scarcity, and I assumed I had shifted it for good. I was wrong.

Abundance is a constant practice, a constant awareness. Scarcity does a bang up job of creeping in when our defenses are down, and when it creeps back in, it can manifest itself very comfortably and begin to alter our behaviour. It will stay there, quite comfortably, until we notice we are in a state of struggle and shift back to an abundant mindset. When I am in a lower vibrating state, if I'm ill or if I'm having a few hard days, I can literally feel the scarcity mindset trying to take over my body. I can feel it trying to break through my barriers and integrate. It's our divine responsibility to pay attention to our inner dialogue to ensure that our thoughts are aligned for abundance, and if they aren't, we have to change the tape and get back in alignment with our higher selves.

In 2014, I was working as a server at a Vancouver restaurant making $8 an hour. This reality ate me alive, because I knew I was designed for more. My inner fire needed to be unleashed, but my deeply rooted security programs bound me. I would finish my serving shift around 1:00 am, rush home, get to bed, and wake up at 5:30 am to start coaching clients, write, and work on the business. For nearly two years, I was getting about five hours of sleep a night. I was terrified of giving up the waitressing job in case Hungry for Happiness completely failed, and I was left homeless. The driving force behind staying at my minimum wage job was fear. As I placed down steak knives and asked the pretentious clientele if they wanted one or two ice cubes in their fancy cocktails, I cringed to think I was serving tables when I needed to be serving the world.

One night, the restaurant was slow, so I decided to lock myself in the bathroom. I shut the door, sat on the floor, and took out my serving notepad from my apron. I obsessively wrote down my mantras and affirmations. After attending three Tony Robbins seminars, I had heard that stuff works like a charm. I kept writing and writing, and tears were streaming from my eyes as my fear overwhelmed my body. The only thing I was waiting on was myself, waiting on myself to make a move, to take a chance. I took the exact same chance on myself when I decided to overcome my eating disorder. I needed to take the step before I saw the staircase. Blind faith.

I left work and walked the four blocks to my apartment, made a cup of tea, and went into my room. I shut the door and sat behind the door staring at my floor length mirror. I stared at myself in the face and saw the tears streaming from my face. I held my chai tea with both hands and felt a sense of comfort.

I mouthed the words, "I trust you" in the mirror. I began to cry harder, and tears were falling in my tea as I repeated myself over and over again. It started as a gentle affirmation and transcended into anger.

"I bloody trust you, Sam!" I yelled at the mirror while I sobbed. After the emotion flowed out, I pulled out my computer and wrote a letter to my manager at the restaurant announcing my resignation.

I burned all my boats. I was cutting off my only reliable source of income and taking a chance on myself. I was ruthlessly committed to creating abundance in my life. I was committed to up leveling and not settling for making $30,000 a year.

In less than twelve months, I went from making $30,000 a year to over $300,000. This was a direct reflection of a shift in mindset and being ruthlessly committed to abundance.

It's important to note here that money is energy. The more energy you attract, the more freedom you have. Your current financial situation is based on your beliefs. If you're in debt and always feeling a sense of "not enough-ness" around money, this is solely based on your beliefs.

I have a dear friend, Emily, who came from an extremely abundant family and was gifted millions of dollars from her family when she was in her mid-twenties. Emily knew that there were people in the world who needed this money more than she did, so she decided to bestow this money upon those in need. Every single penny of her money went to charity. When Emily told me she was committed to donating this money, a small part of me wondered if she would have enough for herself.

Years later, Emily is still more abundant than ever, and continues to attract and give money away to those in need. The point of this story is Emily has an abundance mindset – there are no feelings of lack or limitation with her relationship to money. The wealth that Emily attracts now is not family money, it's self-made, and she continues to find ways to manifest more abundance into her life.

She explained to me that money loves to flow. "You can't be a swamp when it comes to money," she explained to me when we were having tea on a sunny patio in Vancouver one day.

"You need to be a river: give it away, and trust that it is coming back to you."

Taking action in trusting the flow of abundance before you feel ready is a commitment to the universe. You are basically saying, "Ok, I trust you. I am prepared to take the step before I am ready."

For many people, this is absolutely terrifying, and they won't take that first step until they have evidence that they are safe. Again, this isn't the way the world works, and this goes against universal laws. Let it go, release it, and allow it to come back to you with ease.

I have a client in the Hungry for Happiness Society named Jackie, and with her permission, I am sharing this story with you to speak to the fear of living in abundance. Each week in our weekly webinars, the Society members have a chance to share what is coming up for them. I then laser coach them and give them a piece of homework to integrate in the following week. Jackie is a strong willed and strong-minded businessperson who does not believe in any "hippy dippy woo woo shit" – her words, not mine. With this in mind, I knew Jackie was going to have to ease into the truth of abundance. When I was first coaching her through the concept of raising her inner vibrations to attract what she wanted in her life, she stared at me as if I had nine heads. Truthfully, I love working with women who have no concept or reference of working with their inner energy, because when they feel it, they freak out, text me right away, and share their excitement. It's almost like having an orgasm for the very first time!

Jackie's homework was to play with abundance that week, to lean into her desire of what she really wanted, and trust the universe would provide. I told her to start small so she didn't shock her ego or trigger her deeply rooted programs of lack and limitation. Two days later, she sent me a video telling me how she was going on a holiday with her husband to California to watch a tennis match, something they are both passionate about. She told me she was going to test out this abundance thing and stay in a hotel that cost $10,000 a night just to test this whole "energy thing."

After having a little giggle at her message, I sent her one back:

"Jackie, it sounds to me like you are not trusting the universe. You are testing it."

Her message back to me read, "Argh! You got me! I knew you were going to say that." She completely agreed with me and realized that she was acting like a toddler with her power, and rather than fully surrendering and trusting, she was testing, which of course comes from a place of scarcity and skepticism.

We only see what is right in front of us, and the biggest fault in humanity is believing that what we see is all there is. There is so much more at play in our world, which adds to the magic. The magic you are willing to believe and tap into is the amount you will have access to. When we use language to describe it, we create separation within humanity. For many people in the world, the word "God" has negative connotations based on preconceived beliefs. There is a lot of energy around the word God. If it doesn't feel good to you to use that word, then don't, but don't deny the entire energetic field, just because you're hung up on one word, or the meaning of the word.

You are the creator, and you can shift the wording to suit your particular beliefs. God, universe, spirit, higher self, the divine – these are all words that we use to describe the magic we all feel, yet cannot see with the naked eye. Go deeper than word level; we limit ourselves when we are bound by words, and we can easily dismiss the fact that there is something bigger at play.

I threw away the word "God" when I was in my diet depression, because the word didn't resonate with me. In fact, during that time, I didn't have any access to the energetic world, simply because I didn't believe it existed. When I was going through my recovery, I adopted the word "universe" and that felt good to me. Now, the words "God" and "universe" both feel pretty groovy coming out of my mouth.

Choose your own way; choose your own adventure. This is your path, and you have complete freedom. The only thing to note here is that you must believe it in order to feel it.

The shift into an abundant mindset may seem overwhelming and uncomfortable, and perhaps, you are thinking you simply don't have the courage to be able to take on the mission of living in abundance. Perhaps it scares you, perhaps you don't like change, or perhaps you think I'm full of it. I get it; I get it all. I want you to know that you were designed for abundance. You were designed for greatness. Scarcity and struggle are learned behaviours based on the beliefs of society. Our innate state is abundance, bliss, and ease. Again, it's your choice. Choose wisely.

PRACTICE IN ACTION

Scarcity is the root of a lot of evil, especially when it comes to money and food. When you heal your relationship with food, you heal your relationship to money.

Scarcity is at the root of all of this.

When we have the mindset that there isn't enough money, we are constantly worried about it, constantly chasing it, and convinced we will fall short. This creates unneeded stress on the nervous system. When we have the "not enough" mentality with food, we overeat, thinking that it will be our last meal we have on this planet. Scarcity is the driver in obsession, compulsion, and stress. It's essential we transform this deeply rooted belief, otherwise we will never end our fight with food. If you restrict food, chances are you're also restricting money.

EXERCISE #6

Go to the grocery store this week, ask yourself, "What do I really want?" rather than looking to see what is on sale or limiting yourself. Ask yourself what would feel abundant, and purchase that. Don't hold yourself back from what your body wants.

Note that this is not to be confused with the chatter of the mind telling you buy out the isle of Nutella, rather, this is all about tuning into your soul to find out what you truly want at a cellular level. You've been distanced from wanting what you want. You've been living from a place of lack and limitation, and in such an abundant world, that is just not in alignment with truth. You deserve to have exactly what you want. You are enough, and you deserve what you want.

When you've done this, log onto the Phoenix Tribe and tell us what came up for you.

MANTRA

I am enough, I have enough, and I will always have enough.

YOU CAN'T HEAL SOMETHING YOU HATE
Chapter 7

We live in a world where we label emotions as "good" and "bad". We praise the good and we shame the bad. We categorize emotions, and most importantly, we identify with them. When we are experiencing "good" emotions, we desperately hold on to them, hoping they will last forever. When we are on an emotional high, we feel the need to flood our social media feed and let our networks know we feel good. Then, when this emotion falls into a lower vibrating emotion, we immediately jump into judgement, and we judge the fact we are experiencing a low. We then shy away from not only social media, but also the world. We put on a happy face and pretend we are fine, all the while fighting and resisting the pain within our bodies.

What's the issue here? Attachment.

Attachment is the cause of suffering. When we are attached to feeling joy, bliss, and happiness, we completely disregard the beautiful lessons and teachings that are hidden within the so-called "bad" emotions we are experiencing.

Humans avoid pain at all costs, as we tend to numb, distract ourselves from, and suppress the emotions we don't have the courage to face. When these emotions become too strong to suppress with a bag of Doritos, we do our best to shame our way into feeling happy again.

We judge the emotions. We meet them with hate. We equate our self-worth with these "bad" emotions.

Denial is at play here, and when we deny what is, we leave no room to heal what we deny in the first place.

Acceptance of these emotions is the access point to healing them. Hating the pain in your body and fighting it will only strengthen its power and hold over you.

Historically, fighting hate with hate has never worked. To find evidence of this fact, all we need to do is switch on the evening news or read a newspaper. War and religious battles have been using this hate-on-hate modality for centuries, and it only perpetuates the issue.

The issue here is we are making it an issue.

During the four years of my diet depression, I was incessantly filled with shame. I felt like shame was a heavy coat I'd wear that dimmed my light and kept me caged. There was a massive discrepancy between my inner state and who I pretended to be in the world. Shame never took a day off during these four years, nor did it ever shut the hell up and stop telling me I was worthless. It was constantly rattling off derogatory insults, as the voice of shame is loud and clear. It was as if shame stood beside me and screamed bloody murder right into my eardrum.

Shame was so heavy – it was a constriction in my chest and a constant nausea in my stomach. There were days when I craved to be in physical pain in a vain attempt to ignore the emotional pain I was feeling.

My mind always collected data to keep me stuck in the cycle of shame and actively looked for reasons to support the shame story. Our minds are powerful like this. When we have a feeling in our bodies, right away, our mind wants to make meaning of this feeling, create a story around it, and identify with it. Without awareness around how our mind operates, we allow this data to be collected over time, which eventually becomes a massively painful identity we wear around day in and day out. The thought of releasing this story is equally terrifying and exciting.

It's terrifying, because the story becomes our sense of identity and significance, and losing it feels like death to the ego. However, it's also exciting, because it's the feeling of releasing all the mental space, which was held by the story. We get to create a new story.

The weight loss industry has perfected their ability to take advantage of our insecurities to market their products to us. They've mastered the art of manufacturing issues so we can become victims to the industry.

You invest your time, money, and energy, hoping to find freedom from your body issues, but all that happens is you end up overweight and overwhelmed.

As the consciousness of humanity is rising, these quick-fix-Band-Aid-on-a-bullet-wound-solutions will disappear, and humanity will no longer be victim to the diet industry machine – a machine that is constantly churning out false hope.

The next diet plan or miracle pill will not serve you at the level at which you need to be served. It will not heal the pain that resides within your soul. It will only keep you stuck in the diet/binge cycle, stripping you of any semblance of self-love and acceptance you may have. When we succumb to these modalities, we are avoiding the real issue. Fundamentally, we don't believe we have the power and ability to handle the emotions we feel in our bodies; therefore, we distract ourselves by externalizing an internal issue.

The self-hatred you have for your body will not be healed with additional hate. Healing requires intentional self-love to love the painful parts of ourselves. When we can love the parts that need attention, need to be seen, or need approval, we can begin to heal them. You have to feel in order to heal.

Choosing love will only grow love. It doesn't have to be hard – it doesn't have to be a struggle. Struggle is a learned behavior, and it's not innate for us to struggle to grow and live in alignment. You can choose to change the story, use your pain as a catalyst for growth, and expand into the highest, best, and most authentic version of yourself.

Suppressed emotion in the body can create a lot of leverage over us and overwhelm us to the point of extreme anxiety. Whenever we suppress an emotion that needs to be processed and healed, that emotion goes down into the depths of our soul, starts lifting weights and fights back with vengeance. What you fight will strengthen.

Our bodies have a beautiful way of communicating to us that we are off our divine path. When we are off track or playing out programs that aren't aligned with our higher selves, our bodies politely let us know by giving us an intuitive hunch. It starts as a slight tension in our body. It's faint, and if we aren't paying attention we miss it or dismiss it as something else.

When we dismiss it and we don't honour it, the feeling strengthens, and that little hunch in our bellies becomes a knock. The knock sounds like an aggressive neighbour coming over to tell you to shut off your music when it's 11:30 pm. After we decide to ignore this knock, we get the spiritual slap in the face. Essentially, we are knocked on our asses.

We've all been there. Then we convince ourselves our intuition is full of shit. It's only later we confess, "Ahhhh! I should have listened to my intuition the first time!"

Until the lesson is learned and we heal from it, our intuition will keep testing us until we prove we've learned the lesson. Intuition works in miraculous ways. The question is, are you going to surrender and allow the lesson to be easy, or are you going to muscle your way through life getting knocked on your ass repeatedly.

Like everything else, listening to your intuition is a choice. Are you going to let it be easy or are you going to stay stuck in your old pattern and believe that life has to be hard?

Our bodies are fascinating things. When we get injured and blood is pouring from our skin, our body knows exactly how to respond. Blood vessels leading to the wound tighten to reduce the flow of blood to the injured area. Platelets rush to the scene, clumping to each other and adhering to the sides of the torn blood vessel, making a plug. The body does this intuitively – our mind doesn't have to tell our body to respond in this way.

The body is magnificent in its natural healing process. We respond by nurturing, loving, and taking care of the wound so we can speed up the healing process. To transform the skin into its natural state of being, we are connected with it, we do not fight the healing process, and we trust our injury will heal.

Why then, do we adapt a different approach when we are wanting to transform our bodies? When we know that we are holding onto more weight than is comfortable, we take a different approach: we try and shame our way thin. This way of transforming is all based in fear – we use fear, doubt, and hatred to encourage the process of physical change. This process is not only extremely difficult, it isn't sustainable.

It's impossible to heal something you hate.

Your body simply just responded to the demands of your mind. The extra weight on your body is a product of overeating and using food for reasons other than health, hunger, and fuel. The physical weight on your body is a representation of the emotional weight you are carrying. More often than not, the weight on the body was created from a place of fear, which means it's impossible to rid the weight using the very thing that created it: fear.

And it's in this conversation I get the biggest push back from the clients I work with. They fear that if they choose to love their bodies, they would stay complacent and not want to release the weight that isn't serving them. This simply isn't true, in fact it's completely the opposite of how the body works. When we choose to love our bodies, we are able to communicate with them.

Let me explain. Hate, disconnection, and fear block the communication channel from mind and body, head and heart. We aren't able to listen to what our bodies need because we are too busy hating them and trying to fix them. Communication happens when we have connection, and connection can only happen through the process of love and acceptance, not fear and hate. When mind, body, and soul are in harmony, they have the same goal, and they all want to work in perfect unison together, feeding each other information to support the other.

Think of it as a Venn diagram, the two outer circles are mind and body and the circles intersect and meet in the middle, which is the soul. Communication and connection within this triad is the access point to freedom and liberation from the struggle with food and body. It's essential we love the wounded parts so we give them a chance to heal. We must love the extra weight, not only the physical weight, but the emotional weight as well. The more we hate it, the more power the weight has, which only distances us from achieving a three-way harmonious relationship.

It's important to ask your body, "What do you need right now?"

When we can turn our attention inwards and love our inner wounds, only then can they heal. When we can include them and transcend in our growth, everything works with one another, not against. It's time to get curious and love the parts of you that you've previously shamed and denied. Then and only then, will you experience true healing.

One of my greatest joys in life is seeing women come alive, seeing the energetic shift in their bodies when they feel what true, undeniable self-love feels like or the first time they have clear access to their intuition. It's a beautiful moment to witness, and the most exciting part is that you can't unlearn the work of the soul. When you know, you know, and it's yours for keeps.

When women join one of my programs or they join me in an intimate retreat, they are only fixated on the food. They think it's all about the food, which just isn't the case, and they learn this truth very quickly. Food is simply a coping mechanism to numb the pain in their bodies. Locked pain and trauma in the body is the driving force in the fight we have with food. Sometimes hidden trauma that hasn't been healed remains stuck in the body causing havoc and confusion. When we externalize this internal issue and repeatedly fail to overcome the issue, we chalk it up to having no will power, which couldn't be further from the truth.

It's taboo in our society to speak about; however, it's important to shine a light on this very important subject, as there is a world of healing that needs to take place. Remember, we can't heal what we don't feel.

Women come to me all the time who are victims of sexual trauma. More often than not, when they are sharing their experience with me, they tell me that I am one of the only people on the planet who knows they have been through this trauma. When I first started my line of work I was shocked at how many women were suffering with sexual trauma of some sort. Many of these women use the physical weight on their bodies as a barrier to intimacy. Deep within their subconscious mind lies a belief that states, "If I have a physical barrier, I will no longer be vulnerable." This belief is deeply rooted, and usually women don't even know it exists. Once we go through the work and are able to identify this trauma, they begin to heal it.

Most of the time, these sexual traumas happened to my clients before they were 16, and they have been carrying around the shame of that situation since then. For some of the women I work with, this could be nearly 40 years. Forty years of hiding, feeling like a victim, and feeling unsafe in their feminine body. The pain is both emotional and physical, and the work towards healing starts as soon as we can voice the pain, speak to it, and lean into it. The hardest part of this process is leaning into the pain, learning to be with it, and not separate ourselves from it.

Separation is the birthplace of all anxiety in the body, and we need to include this part of us in the totality of our beings. Denial of what is will only perpetuate the emotional pain. When we can accept it, love it, and lean into it with a full heart, we are able to move through it. This process is simple, but it isn't easy. It takes courage, bravery, and immense support to be able to fully dive into these parts of ourselves. There is immense fear digging deep. Women fear if they bring it up or acknowledge it that it will happen again. We reclaim our power by shining the light on it. The only way is through.

Trauma survivors who develop patterns of binge eating are fogged from reality and inundated with confusion. When we lift the veil and get real with what is, we develop an awareness, which can be healed with acceptance, love, and connection. Trauma survivors are afraid to feel, and when we don't feel, we don't have the access to heal. When we are not acting out from a place of self-love, we are committing violence against ourselves. It's one or the other; each action we take throughout the day is either in alignment with the highest version of ourselves or is in violation of our highest self.

When we are tuned in with our bodies and nourishing our bodies at the deepest level, we are acting from a place of self-love. When we are numbed out, distracted, and shoveling food in our mouths, we are committing violence towards our bodies. Women who have history of sexual trauma are validating their experiences by using food as a tool to strengthen the story they've created around the violence. Even though the reality is a painful one, we know it well, and we continue to add leverage to the story we've created in our minds. Spending time with the little child within us who experienced this trauma and uniting her with your adult self allows this healing process to take place. Unity, connection, and love will heal all.

You are not your past, and at your core is a perfect being of light and love. You can't change the wrong that was done to you, but you can certainly allow yourself to heal from it. Once we have awareness, we get to practise responsibility. When we know there is a deep part of us that needs healing, we have to take responsibility for showing up for ourselves, doing the deep inner work from a place of compassion and love to release all that is not serving us. You are not your story. You are a powerful woman who is capable of using this as a chance to use your pain as the catalyst for deep growth and expansion.

PRACTICE IN ACTION

When we hate our bodies, we don't give them a chance to heal.

When we avoid our emotions, we have no data to help us find out what we need to lean into and love. Connection creates communication. When we are connected to our bodies and we deeply love ourselves, we are able to honour and trust our intuition and create deeper agreements with our bodies. We learn that our body has our back, no matter what. Whether it's with food, relationships, money, or men – we always know the answer.

Most of the time when I work with clients, and we are talking about intuitive eating they say to me, "But Sam, when I eat whatever I want, I go right for the cookies."

If this is the case for you, you're still listening to your mind.
There is a huge difference.

The mind is busy, and it likes to negotiate, to complicate decisions.

The body is a deep, profound knowing. There is no arguing, because its needs are clear.

EXERCISE #7

In this exercise I want you to get clear about the difference between a "yes or no" from the mind and a "yes or no" from the body. The goal is to connect to your body so it can tell you exactly what it needs. To start with, I just want you to know the difference between "yes" and "no" in your body.

Think of a question that has a definite "yes" answer.

For example, "Is my name Sam?" or "Do I love tacos?" (Replace tacos with whatever you want; I really love tacos.)

Close your eyes and ask yourself the question. Repeat it multiple times until you feel the energetic shift in your body. A "yes" in the body feels calm, light, uplifting, almost like opening the double French doors to the seaside. It's certain.

Now, think of a definite "no" question.

For example, "Am I a man?" or "Do I live in Mexico?" (Unless you live in Mexico, choose a different country.)

Close your eyes and ask yourself this question. Repeat it multiple times until you feel the energetic shift in your body. A "no" can feel heavy, sinking, or tight.

This part is critical to ending the fight you have with food and your body. If you feel complete numbness in your body when you do this exercise, then I want you to stay with this practice until you can feel the difference on a visceral level. Connecting to the body to hear its guidance is profound, and you deserve to give yourself this gift.

Stay with it – you will get there.

After years of being disconnected, this may take a few weeks to feel, but you will get there. It's important with this kind of work to not hustle for it. If it's not happening right away, simply accept that. As soon as you make it a problem, you will create inner disconnect and chaos, the very thing we are looking to heal.

MANTRA

I am in the process of listening to, honouring, and trusting my body.

MY BODY BREAKDOWN
Chapter 8

"You want me to love the one thing I've been hating for years on end?"

It's as if my therapist was asking me to climb Mount Everest. Actually no, I would have done that – I'd be motivated by how many calories I could burn. My therapist insisted I get to know my body, the very thing I had been running from, the very thing I'd sworn I would never love for as long as I walked the earth. It was impossible.

Coming back into my body was harder than passing Math 12, and trust me, that was a struggle in itself. I'd make up all sorts of clever excuses to miss math class, but my teacher knew my tactics and wouldn't let me get away with any of it. I remember trying to pass Math being the hardest feat of my life, until now.

This was harder. This was terrifying. I didn't know what was on the other side of this hatred I had for my body. The uncertainty felt like someone was choking me, and I felt the anxiety ball in my throat. I could have sworn if I didn't tell myself to breathe, I would suffocate to death.

After being at war with something for so long, making peace with it is a bittersweet process, riddled with doubt and uncertainty. I had to befriend my body, I had to love it, and I had to learn to trust it again. But I had been doing everything in my power for the longest time to do the complete opposite. I was on a mission to hate it more, damage it, change it, and abuse it. It was as if World War III was happening between my mind and my body. It was time for a ceasefire and to make peace.

Everything in my life was carefully manufactured to support the battle with my body. I bought clothes that were too small, hoping to fit into them when I found a diet that worked. I had two large scales (one in the bedroom, one in the bathroom), a mini scale in my purse, and a mini scale in the kitchen. My environment was set up in a way to support the battle with my body, and I truly believed changing my external world to represent where I wanted to be was going to work. I thought I was a one smart cookie.

As far as the scale of Body Dysmorphic Disorder goes, I was at the far, severe end of the spectrum. I would look in the mirror and see a completely different person, a completely different body. There was no correlation between the number on the scale, how I looked in the mirror, and how I felt in my body. I couldn't understand why I hated my body so much. What had happened? Where did this come from? I was in constant denial, but I kept ignoring my hatred and just powered through and used restrictive diets to deal with the pain I was feeling in my body. If I just damaged my body, it would numb the pain I feel in my body. I wanted to numb the pain I felt when I looked in the mirror, put on clothes, or got out of the shower. I'd justify my disgust by telling myself, "It's ok. I am dieting. Soon this will all change."

I was constantly running from what was, what I saw, and how I felt, never making peace with reality, never facing it. Always avoiding it. This is how I would save myself from emotional breakdowns. My mind would begin racing and figuring what I needed to do to get to my goal weight more quickly.

For years I thought I needed to shame myself skinny, and the harder I was on my body, the skinnier I would be. When I started to feel at ease in my body, I would crack down on the shame, making sure I didn't slip into being comfortable, because being comfortable meant gaining 300 pounds in a week. I couldn't see the part in me that was worthy of being respected.

This is one of the most common things I hear from the women I work with on my retreats and in my programs: "But Sam, there is nothing to respect. There is nothing to love - I am fat and hideous."

Women think they are fundamentally flawed. They see no truth, no beauty, and especially no love. Breaking free of this fallacy, allowing themselves to feel inner love is at first like telling them water is not wet. They don't get it, and they think I'm smoking something. They are so attached to the part of themselves that they believe is broken, they don't believe that within them exists a place that is pure love, a place that is desperate for love, a place that has never let them down and only wants them to vibrate at the highest level. This place is beyond the weight, beyond the fear, and beyond what the logical mind can even comprehend.

I explain to these women that fundamentally, we were all designed to be happy and to love ourselves. When you were a child you never once questioned your worth while you were swinging from the monkey bars after school. You demanded what you wanted and didn't feel guilty about it. There was never a correlation between the size of your body and your self-worth.

I remember going into the kitchen, claiming my power, and demanding from my mom that I have a cookie. I knew, without a doubt, that cookie was mine. I didn't care about anything else. I stood my ground and asked for what I wanted, without holding back, or questioning my worth. More often than not, I got what I wanted. And I didn't justify what I wanted to anyone.

As we grow up, we feel the need to justify the desires of our heart or our body. We always throw in a "because" so those around us don't think that we are selfish, greedy humans. You're allowed to just want what you what because you want it: no explanation needed, no justification. Listen to your heart, acknowledge your desires and just ask for it - no holding back. What is good for you is good for the world.

I lay on my bathroom floor, where I spent a lot of my time during my diet depression, and looked into a handheld mirror and cried. I can remember the feeling so vividly. I wanted to crawl out of my skin, to shed my body off as if I were a snake shedding its skin. After all, I was born in the year of the snake, and on same level I kind of thought shedding the body I hated might be possible.

My mind was mighty, and if it had the potential to think my beautiful 125 pound body was the size of a Japanese sumo wrestler, I'm sure it could handle this. That is something I did know for certain: I have the manifestation power of a magician. I lay there on the ground, feeling the cold blue tile through my t-shirt and the anxiety flowing throughout my entire body – a vicious steam of energy overtaking me with vengeance. I lay there and wondered if this was ever going to end.

My mind wandered to a place it hadn't been in a while. What was that feeling actually like – the feeling of loving my body? I brought myself back to the time I felt the most powerful, aligned, and loveable. It was 2006, and I was competing in Canadian National Dance Championships, doing a duet with my best friend Lauren. Our dance was choreographed to "Behind the Wall," a dark, introspective song about two women facing serious trauma. These two women don't know each other, they just experience each other's lives through their single, shared wall. Lauren and I represented these women. The song was heart-wrenching, and I danced to represent the pain of women facing abuse worldwide. Every time I performed this number, tears would stream down my face, and I felt as if I was shredding the pain and weight of abused women, raising the feminine consciousness with each performance. Energy raced through my body with each kick, triple turn, and grande jeté. I felt bold. I felt fearless. I felt alive.

I allowed myself to marinate in this energy for a moment, reliving the power that my body represented on that stage.

Holy hell I thought. I could breathe, my brain fog cleared, and in this moment, I was able to feel lightness. My mind was dictating my feelings – what a concept. For years now, I had allowed my mind to lure me into states of anxiety, fear, doubt, and self-hatred. For this moment, as I lay on that bathroom floor, I was able to rekindle the feelings of purity, lightness, and power.

Unintentionally, my breath deepened, and as I breathed in and out, I could feel my entire body surrendering into the floor. For the first time in a long time, I felt completely liberated, completely at ease. This moment was a turning point, as it was first time I recognized the power I had to shift my inner vibrations. I felt high, as if I'd just downed a few magic mushrooms. Knowing my mind created this experience and shifted this feeling within a matter of minutes was incredible.
Suffering is learned behaviour. We are not designed to suffer. God didn't create us to be on this planet and live in a constant state of hating ourselves. We have picked it up from our parents, our parents' parents, and our parents' parents' parents...you get the point.

Fundamentally, at our core, we are designed for happiness and expansion. Here is the deal: those programs that are running your life create utter chaos in your mind and have been adapted into your experience. They aren't a part of you. You are creating a warm, cozy, bed for them.

They are fucking painful, yet oddly comfortable, so you hold onto them, and they run you and keep you in a state of suffering to distance you from the highest, best, and most authentic version of who you are.

Now, before you get depressed and think this is your reality, hear me out. You have everything it takes to detach from these programs, create new ones, and change the trajectory of your entire life. Within you is the power and ability to recognize these patterns and change your core beliefs at a visceral and cellular level to change your entire life. You might be thinking that this is "hippy dippy woo woo shit," but stay with me.

Our lives are manufactured by our beliefs. At a deep core level, we believe we are not good enough. When we fundamentally believe we aren't good enough, we then create thoughts around this belief.

I will never be able to be happy.
I will never have the man I want.
I will never be in the body I desire.

These thoughts then create feelings in our body: shame, guilt, anxiety, and doubt. When we are vibrating at a low level, if affects our actions, our results, and the quality of our lives. Everything starts with a core belief — absolutely everything.

If you want to change your life, you have to change your beliefs.

It's not enough to stare at yourself in the mirror and repeat, "I am enough. I am enough. I am enough." Don't get me wrong, affirmations are the bee's knees, but unless you viscerally connect to the feeling, you might as well be saying, "The sky is blue. The sky is blue. The sky is blue." It has no leverage, no emotional connection. You have to attach to the feeling of worth on a visceral level, creating a link in the brain between the affirmation and the feeling. The best part about settling into the feeling of worthiness is the fact that it's our natural state.

We all know how to feel worth. Yes, you might have been riding on the self-hatred train for 10, 20, maybe even 30 years, but self-hatred is not innate, it's learned. Get off at the next stop, because the train is headed to hell. You have to understand and embody the feeling of worth without reason, without external factors, or without any justification.

Just like the kid with the cookie, you deserve to feel how you want, just because. And I get it, we live in a world that glorifies the connection between worth and accolades. There always has to be a reason. We find it hard to create this feeling "just because." You get to feel worthy, just because that is a universal law – how cool is that?

You know when you buy a new car and you see that damn car everywhere? Before owning the car, you were completely oblivious to the fact that it was even on the planet, and now you can't bloody drive down the road without seeing the same car. Discovering your worth is no different. As soon as you decide to claim your worth (right in this very moment for example), you will start to see examples and evidence of your worth everywhere. When you program your mind in this manner, you can't help but look for evidence. In fact, you don't even have to look, because your mind does a brilliant job of finding the evidence for you.

Just like for the last however many years your mind has been finding reasons why you don't deserve to feel worthy, and when you collect evidence to support this idea, your mind has a celebration: "Ha! I told you, you worthless piece of meat! I told you I'm right!" We've all been there. Our minds are on default mode, searching for leverage to make the story even bigger and badder.

So, let's zone in on something for just a hot minute. You will get frustrated, you will get annoyed, and you will want to throw in the towel and jump right back on that self-hatred train. Why? Because for years, your mind has been busy building up this story, and we're going to come along and take a sledgehammer to it and smash it. It will feel like death. In fact, it is. Part of you is dying – the small part of you trying to keep you "safe" is dying. Will it be a little painful? Yup. Will you want to back down? Absolutely. Will you? That is your choice, but do you want to prolong your suffering or commit to your greatness?

The purpose of life is to expand – we gotta go, girl. If we don't, life will do it for us. Think about it: everything in life grows and expands – the universe, people, social structures – everything. If we don't grow and follow the laws of the universe, life will do it for us. And it normally comes in the form of a smack to the face. It winds up and just hits us right across the chops. We can suffer our way to that growth, or we can be proactive and take ownership and responsibility over our growth.

At the moment, your higher self is devastated that you hate your body. She is watching you with her face in her hands, shaking her head. She is giving you signs and signals all day long, but you're not listening. Self-hatred and body loathing blocks the communication from not only your intuition, but your higher self. You feel alone, unsupported, and alienated.

During my recovery from my diet depression, I was told to accept my body. Accept my body? Are you fucking nuts?!?!

I silently screamed at Ray, "Ha! That is a hilarious joke! How can I accept my body when I'm not at my ideal weight?"

I sat there thinking that damn therapy session was a waste of time and money. I sat there thinking that this grey-haired man was losing it – he didn't understand. Maybe I'll find acceptance when I am at my ideal weight: the goal I had in my mind. I was ten pounds away from it. Until then, my plan was to shame myself skinny. That made the most logical sense in my mind.

I could feel my rage, my panic, and my frustration boil through my skin. I looked up at the clock. Thank god, I thought. There were only three minutes left of this damn session before I could go home and figure out how to shed the last ten pounds from my body. I sat there for the next few moments nodding my head and bold-faced lying when I told him I'd give it a go. I chuckled at the thought of accepting myself, the thought of looking in a mirror and smiling. What a concept.

After months of telling Ray I was doing my homework, I finally came clean. I finally told him I couldn't hack this whole acceptance thing. I looked back at the last few months: same weight, same hatred, same frustration. I know I am stubborn, but I was just being stupid. Here I was paying someone for advice, not listening, and not seeing any results. My logical brain was finally activated and spoke up: "Ok Sam, get your shit together. This is getting ridiculous!"

I felt a dull pain in my stomach, and I wanted to barf all over Ray's couch. Thankfully, I didn't, but this visceral pain was the universe giving me good ol' smack in the face, because I chose to make this hard on myself. I was riddled with fear at the thought of accepting myself, and I immediately went to the worst-case scenario: accepting myself and gaining 300 pounds in the process.

No boys would ever date me, I'd have to fly business class, because I wouldn't fit in the normal seats, and I would have to get rid of all my clothes. That's where my mind went.

Being the headstrong, stubborn, women I that am, I finally decided to fully commit to this acceptance thing, despite the fact it terrified me. I looked at my track record of hating my body and realized that it really wasn't working for me. The whole "just one more diet" thing just really wasn't panning out. I was left lost, confused, and totally frustrated with myself.

I left Ray's office and walked the twenty minutes it took to get home. In typical Vancouver fashion, it was raining as I contemplated how I was going to start accepting myself. For the first time I realized the severity of my battle. It was now or never: this needed to end, and it ends now - no more fighting, no more sugarcoating the battle.

It's done.
It's over.
It ends now.

I woke up the next morning with a new story in my mind. I looked in the mirror and said out loud, "Ok Sam, we are going to accept our body today, whatever that looks like."
I giggled to myself, feeling doubt and excitement, as the contract I had made with myself was comical. I stared at myself with wonder – wonder about what this journey would look like, wonder about who I really was, and wonder what life will be like on the other side of this pain.

For the first time in a long time I felt peace. I felt ease, simply from just making a decision to learn how to accept my body. Thank God for my mother, who taught me the power of decisive decision-making. That woman doesn't budge for nothing. When her mind is made up, consider it gospel. There is no negotiation.

I was committed. I was determined to rebuild the personal integrity I had demolished over the last few years. I had broken every promise I had made to myself, destroyed my self-trust, and allowed myself to damage my mind and body without care. Thinking about this brought tears to my eyes. It was time to show up for myself, it was time to show myself what integrity meant, and it was time to trust my beautiful body once again.

As the weeks went on, I began to make little promises to myself, and I would follow up with action. Each time I did this, I knew I was rebuilding my trust, and I'd do a little air fist pump and carry on with my day. These things were small, little agreements I'd create in the morning to ensure I was keeping my word and living in alignment with my higher self.

"Today I commit to eating mindfully and listening to my body."
"Today I commit to smiling at myself as I pass mirrors."
"Today I commit to being curious about the anxiety I am feeling, not stuff it with food."
"Today I commit to feeling worth in each moment."
"Today I commit to being playful."

Whatever it was, I created something I knew I could follow through with by the end of the day. This feeling was liberating, and I felt accomplished. My god, this acceptance thing was awesome.
I leaned further and further into it as the months went by. I explored the edge of my acceptance, and I noticed how at ease I would feel in situations that usually triggered me – social engagements for instance. I was in awe how peaceful acceptance felt and in awe of the power I was able to cultivate in my body.

I realized something extremely powerful. Acceptance is not synonymous with complacency. Read that again. Acceptance is not synonymous with complacency.

Just because you accept yourself, does not mean you are going to stay stuck. It does not mean you are going to gain 300 pounds and be forced to take business class because you can't fit in an economy sized seat.

Acceptance allows transformation to happen at our deepest level. When we are truly accepting of ourselves, we are able to transform from a place of ease, lightness, and peace. It must start from love. It must start from accepting reality. No matter how heavy you are, how much weight you have to lose, how much shame you feel, it starts with acceptance. From there, we can take inspired action and transform into the highest, best, and most authentic versions of ourselves.

In order to learn what acceptance felt like, I had to quiet my mind by getting present to the moment. And yes, I had to "sit in the shit" – sit with those sticky emotions I'd been running from for years. I had to stop pretending I was so busy and realize my busyness was keeping me from feeling my feelings.

We praise busyness in our society. We hustle and bustle around on the proverbial hamster wheel, distancing ourselves from feeling our truth and hearing the calls of our souls. In the midst of one task, we are already thinking of the next four we need to accomplish before we lay our heads down on the pillow in preparation to do it all again the next day. We live by to-do lists and checkboxes, searching for validation and worthiness through a false sense of productivity. We turn our lives into a race with no finish line. There's no prize at the end, not even a measly participation ribbon.

We have to stop hustling for our worth.

The world is coming around to the concept of meditation, with plenty of studies worldwide confirming the impact meditation has on our brains and our bodies, infusing more peace, compassion, and acceptance into our lives.

The resistance and excuse I hear most often from my clients when I suggest trying this life altering practice is, "I'm too busy." They confess they couldn't possibly create the space and time in their day to sit in lotus position and calm their thoughts while focusing on being present. Meditation is not exclusive to this position, and you do not need to lock yourself in a dark room chanting "Om" undisrupted for hours on end until you finally find the desired level of Zen you're after.

There is a beautiful thing I called Integrative Meditation, which is taking meditative concepts and applying them to your day and to the energy of your essence. This is a form of meditation that isn't as mainstream as the classic picture of meditation we have in our minds when the word arises. Meditation is merely engaging in mental exercise, such as concentrating on one's breathing or repeating a mantra, for the purpose of reaching a heightened level of spiritual awareness. Nowhere in this description does it say you need to be in alone in a dark room sitting in lotus position to meditate.

The divine practice of Integrative Meditation introduces the concept of shifting perception in your day to evoke an altered energy within the body that brings forth more awareness, thus connecting deeper into the soul.

This practice is rooted in the concept of presence: being hyper-aware to one's surroundings, feelings, and emotions while completing everyday tasks. This takes no extra time, only a shift in perception.

Let's try this right now. As you are reading the words on the page, I want you to feel into your body. Keep reading as you feel. As you continue to read, take a moment and notice your breath. Notice how it feels in your body when you deepen your breath. As you continue to read and deepen your breath, I want you to notice how you are feeling. What is the state of your emotional landscape?

Continue to read as you notice your breath and observe how you are feeling, right here in this very moment. You just experienced a total state change, you went from reading this book and just trying to get through it, to reading with intention while you focused on how your body was feeling. This is a brief example of the magic of Integrative Meditation.

Now, imagine yourself bringing this same energy and awareness to the things you do in your day – the seemingly mundane and insignificant tasks you complete each day. When we can bring our whole selves to each moment and bring meaning to each moment, we create a totally different experience by not changing our external actions at all. When we can wake up to this reality, our lives shift, we become more present, more aware, calmer, and more connected. In this state, we drastically change our behaviours. We are in complete control to shift our internal worlds by simply bringing awareness to the present moment. It's a beautiful and innate practice that we've distanced ourselves from. Coming back to this state of hyper-awareness will require us to keep our consciousness from reverting back to the hamster wheel. But when this mindful practice is engrained in the body, we will slip into it with ease, because living this way is how we were fundamentally designed to operate.

Tony Robbins, one of my home boys (he doesn't know I call him that), talks about NET – no extra time – which is the process of developing personal practices that don't require you to quit your job to complete them. Integrative Meditation follows this principle. Rather than zoning out and thinking about everything but what you are currently doing (meditating), you get to immerse yourself in the task at hand while you meditate, which not only helps you complete the task with a heightened state of awareness, but allows you to strengthen your mind-body connection whilst doing it.

The beauty in this process is that it's available to you at all times. Your conscious mind is always there waiting for you to fully utilize it to evoke a state change. When we have the power and ability to change our states, we have the power and ability to change our lives. As I mentioned in previous chapters, my resistance to meditation was huge. Sitting cross-legged in lotus position made me want to throw myself off a building. When I realized that I could take an alternative approach to meditation, I was giddy with excitement.

I can remember my first stab at it. I was standing in front of my sink, staring at the pile of dishes that accumulated from the vegetarian lasagna I just made and gulped down. I can remember the all-so-common anxiety I felt after eating anything during my diet depression. I decided I was going to calm my mind and body down completely. I felt into my feet, feeling the steady ground under my feet and had a felt sense of gratitude for my feet. They had been supporting me in my journey for my entire life. I worked my attention up through my body. I scanned my legs, focusing on how it was a miracle they were able to complete all I asked of them.

I was present in my body, observing my physical pains, and noticing my emotional pains. I felt into my heart, and I asked it what it needed. I noticed a sadness, as if my heart was crying. I was able to not worry about pushing the sadness away, but simply love it, love the pain, love the sadness. I felt my breath deepen as I paid more and more attention to my body and what it was communicating to me in that very moment. I felt alive. I decided I was simply just going to observe how I was feeling and where I was, with no intention to change it or numb it – just simply be with it. This was a foreign concept to me, as all of my life I've been on a constant quest to get somewhere or do something. But now, I just got to be with it all, experience it all, and love it all. I felt connected to my body. I felt liberated from the anxiety and guilt I felt just five minutes earlier.

I felt the warm, soapy water on my hands. I had a deep sense of gratitude for the water, and I took a moment to realize how fortunate I was to have running water, just by simply turning on a tap. How blessed was I? I had been given this beautiful gift of running water when a large population of the planet had to travel miles for a bucket full of water, then carry it on their heads back to their villages, and here I am with it at my disposal. I thought about the food I'd just eaten, how it was nourishing my body, how the food was traveling through my body and the nutrients were being absorbed to nourish my body so it can run effectively and beautifully.

I let my mind wonder further and thought about how far the food had to travel to get to me. I had a felt sense of gratitude for all the humans who were involved in picking this food, preparing it, washing it, exporting it – whatever needed to be done in order for it to be on my plate. I took time to send love to all these people. What an honour and blessing it was that I am able to effortlessly go to the grocery store and simply buy food to eat. During this time of intense concentration, I felt a wave of relief, as if the world, as well as my heart, had completely cracked open. I felt clear, I felt alive, and I feel empowered. The thought of "life is supposed to be easy" flooded my consciousness as my body sunk deeper and deeper into a relaxed state. This was going on all while I was just standing there at my sink, washing the dishes.

Just moments earlier, I was feeling exhausted and overwhelmed. I was thinking of the next four things I needed to do before bed, while obsessing over how many calories were in the lasagna and how many hours of cardio I needed to do to burn it off in the morning. I was completely out of alignment with my higher self.

But through the exercise, I became conscious of the beautiful blessings that were so obviously right in front of me. I had been consumed with the obsession of what was next. This is how we spend most of our lives. We are always on a quest to get somewhere, be someone, or change something about ourselves. When we deny what is, we have no power to transcend it.

At one of my retreats, one of the participants said to me, "I know when I feel my intuition I won't be miserable anymore, but I'm still waiting."

As soon as those words came out of her mouth, she knew she had it backwards. She could tell by the look on my face that I was able to give her a dose of tough love.

I looked at her lovely face and said, "If that is your thought pattern, you will be miserable for the rest of your life."

I explained to her that by virtue of believing this thought, she was blocking the flow of miracles into her life. When we are in a miserable state waiting for things to change we are attached to an external outcome. This is a classic, and an ever-so-common case of "when-then-it is": When I lose X pounds, then I will feel Y. When we play the "when-then" game, we are denying what is in the moment. When we deny what is, we simply don't have the ability to accept and move on. You can't create sustainable transformation from a place of hatred and fear. You can't heal something you hate.

Try it on for size. Embody the essence of peace now. You have all the power and ability within you to create the transformation your heart desires. Stop waiting on the weight.

PRACTICE IN ACTION

Befriending my body was one of the most terrifying, yet liberating, things I've ever done in my life. I've never been skydiving, but I can imagine it would go something like this: "Shit! I'm in this plane. I have to do jump. There is no other option."

I literally had no other option.

I had to observe what hating my body was costing me and do something about it. It was do or die.

EXERCISE #8

In this exercise, I want you to write a love letter to your body. Let her know you're ready to love her and ready to end the battle. It's time to connect into your soul and be one with your being.

Then, and only then, will you find freedom with the fight you have with food and your body. When we have connection with our bodies, we also have communication. We are able to speak to our bodies, and our bodies have a channel to speak to us. This is the sweet spot. Without this, it's impossible to end the fight you have with food.

It's time to take yourself on a date. Plan a night to do this and commit to having a couple hours to yourself. Have a bath, light some candles, make some tea – do whatever you need to do to feel the essence of inner peace and self-love.

Start writing to your body, and share whatever comes to mind. Share your truth, say sorry, and tell her you're ready to love her.

Thank her for constantly having your back while you disowned her and treated her terribly.

This process is emotional, you might even tear up even thinking about doing this. This is beautiful —allow the emotion to flow – it's been trapped in there for years.

Again, as always, if you feel called to, share your letter with the Phoenix Tribe.

You've got this.

MANTRA

I love, honour, and respect my beautiful body.

RAISING YOUR STANDARDS
Chapter 9

You need to give yourself permission to want what you want. This is an essential piece to transforming not only your mind, but your body as well. Owning the journey of lightness with absolute certainty you will achieve all desire is the foundation to ending the battle with your body. You are a magnificent being. You were created perfectly whole. You were not given less than any other human on this planet. You were given everything you need to become all you desire.

What do you really want? What really makes you happy?

One of the biggest reasons that you overindulge with food, is because you are depriving yourself in other areas. Your way of making up for this emotional deprivation is overeating and getting your fix through food. That inner need is not met, because you've decided you're not worthy of it. It's not possible to get what you want, so why bother trying? This unmet need has manifested itself in your relationship with food; therefore, you overeat to "fill up" what you've failed to meet at a core level.

Many of us are extreme people pleasers, and we will go out of our way to make someone else happy, even if it means we are putting ourselves last. We are so terrified of not being liked and accepted that we ensure the needs of others are met before our own. This pattern reinforces that we aren't worthy of asking for and getting exactly what we want in our lives. We don't believe we are worthy or that it's possible for us to achieve what we want. This belief is completely contradictory to how we are supposed to live and thrive on this planet.

It's our birthright on this planet to ask for exactly what we want.

It's our birthright to feel the way we want to feel and be in the bodies that make us the most comfortable. It's not your genes that are the problem here. It's your decision to believe you're not worthy of lightness. You are the only one getting in the way. You are the one who is suppressing your desires with food and playing the victim card. This is a hard truth, but one that needs to be fully realized before we can transcend it into higher vibrating realities. You, my dear, are the creator of that place.

First, we need to feel our worth, feel it fully with our whole hearts, our whole bodies – the feeling of lightness and peace, where the inner chaos is alkalized and we are living in alignment with our truth. The beautiful thing here is we are able to reach that place energetically, without dropping a pound. We aren't running from our bodies, rather, we are embracing them and raising our inner energy to match that of which we want to attract.

This is how we manifest – from a place of pure love and focused intention. In this place, it's essential you expect miracles, and you expect them to come to you with ease. When we raise our inner vibrations, it makes it so much easier to allow miracles to flow into our lives and manifest in our bodies. Fear and doubt block this flow from occurring, and when we don't believe we are worthy of weight release, we are telling the universe to not support us in making it happen.

How much joy are you going to allow yourself to experience? This is where the process becomes fun, because we get to engage our imagination and play with the possibility of becoming the highest, best, and most authentic versions of ourselves. By virtue of simply focusing on the possibilities, we get to interact and converse with the truth of who we are.

When we allow ourselves to dream and put ourselves in this place of exploration, we can interact with the truest part of who we are. When we feel into this space with clarity from a place of being grounded, it's freeing. When we allow ourselves to dance in the magic of creation from a place of truth, it feels like home. We've all felt this place, and for most of us, this place was when we were much younger. Sometimes when we are extremely happy as adults, we get glimpses of this energy: it's expansive and beautiful.

Want what you want with all your heart, celebrate the victory before it happens, and align yourself with the energy of achieving what you want.

Lean into the desire and notice the doubts that come up when you are in your creative space.

"You're not worthy."
"You're way too fat to think you can be beautiful."
"Yeah, right. That will take liposuction to get there."

Whatever comes up for you, notice it, allow it to be in your body, and ask yourself how true it really is. Generally, these fears that hold us back from our greatness are simply just stories we've been telling ourselves for years that hold no merit or leverage. As untrue and uncomfortable as they feel in our body, we are certain they are true. We've always believed them, we continue to reinforce the pattern, time and time again.

We are operating under stories that aren't even our own. We are keeping a safe warm bed for these stories while they are busy holding us back from our truth and who we really are.

Chew on that for a moment. It's a depressing truth, and it's one that is counterintuitive to how we were created. There are a lot of higher-selves shaking their heads in dismay right now saying, "Girl, you are so damn powerful. Start acting like it!" As soon as we can own this part of ourselves, we can start acting like it.

We suffer when we live below our potential. When we act out behaviours that are not in alignment with our truth, we can feel it weighing down our hearts, but we repeat the pattern, because we've not yet raised our standards. We hit resistance when we try to transform our lives without raising our standards. We binge on self-help books and other recourses without digging into the deep emotional reason as to why we don't want to change. Having low standards about what you will tolerate, while trying desperately to be a better person, will only keep you on the hamster wheel: blaming the system, the facilitator, the work – everything and everyone, except the person in the mirror.

On some level we want someone to do the work for us. We want to plug into a source of power and channel the gods to change our lives for us. I'm sorry to be the bearer of bad news, but this isn't going to happen, my dear.

Let's be real for a moment. You've lived your whole life under the same low standards you have now.

This isn't going to change unless you actively change it — unless you know in your heart you deserve more, you deserve to no longer struggle, to no longer feel the weight that comes with self-sabotage. Until then, nothing will change.

Raising your standards starts with a profound knowing that you are a child of the universe; therefore, you deserve greatness, light, and love in abundant amounts. You deserve to be aligned with your higher self, feel how you want to feel, do what you want to do, and live how you want to live. Until you realize these truths, you will stay stuck. Until you realize you are a limitless being, capable of moving mountains and becoming the highest, best, and most authentic version of yourself, you will continue to play out the story of "I'm not good enough." And you will attract things, people, and experiences that are aligned with that core belief, because nothing changes without changing the belief. Taking note of where your standards are now, without judgement, will ultimately allow you to live in alignment with your highest self.

If you wake up and your first thought of the day is one that crushes your soul, you have low standards — end of story. This was my life, for years. The first thought that would dance through my mind in the morning was either guilt from what I did the night before or that I was too disgusting to wear what I actually wanted to wear that day. Anchoring that thought in the morning set the tone for my entire day. My powerful mind, which took a concept and ran with it, coupled with the low standards for what I allowed in my life created a recipe for inner destruction.

During one of my coaching sessions with Ray, he asked me about my personal standards. I squinted my eyes at him in pure confusion, and had no idea what this man was talking about. He proceeded to tell me that my life was a result of my standards — what I was willing to settle for. His statement slapped me across the face in the best way possible.

Immediately, I was like, "My god, I don't think I even HAVE standards."

I went home distraught from my therapy session that day. Once upon a time, I had standards coming out of my ass, and now I'd completely lost touch with them. This battle with food had stripped me of my standards. I would have thrown myself under a bus for a brownie.

This awareness was painful, yet eye-opening. It was incredible to have the fog lifted for me to see clearly how I'd been destroying certain parts of my life. It wasn't just my relationship with food, but because that was my biggest issue, it was leaking into the majority of my life.

I rode my bike back to my apartment, opened the front door, and wanted to raid the fridge after having this painful realization.

Standards, standards, standards!

My mind raced. I felt trapped. All I wanted to do was dive into the pantry, but I knew I needed to sit with this pain. I ran to my room, slammed the door, and threw myself on my bed. I began sobbing, and tears streamed from my face and soaked my pillow. Usually this would be the time that I would suppress my emotion with food, but not this time. I let myself go. I let myself breakdown. This is what I needed.

I stared up to the white ceiling, and I felt a sense of relief. The pain had subsided. In fact, there were no emotions at all. I felt peace. Peace was a feeling I'd had been craving for years – the sense of inner peace and the calming sensations that come from a mind that isn't constantly activated. I continued to just lie there, silently. I could feel my eyes widen as I connected deeper and deeper into my body. I kept myself calm by assuring myself I was safe. I was doing one of the most natural things a human can do: lie down and breathe, but there was a part of me that was completely terrified. Feeling connected with my body after years of fighting it was unlike anything I ever imagined.

I untucked myself from the fetal position and placed both feet on the floor. I looked straight ahead, and there was my vision board. I caught a glimpse of a woman in lotus position. She looked peaceful. She looked how I felt. I stood up from my bed, walked over to the mirror, and just stared at myself.

I felt like I was staring back at my truth. My eyes were clear, and my heart was light. I mouthed the words "I love you" in the mirror. This statement shocked my body, as I was feeling such drastic contrast in my emotional field. I stayed with it, and it was as if I was learning to walk again. Feeling it out, being careful not to disrupt this state, I touched the mirror and just stared at myself. While I felt like I was tripping on some sort of psychedelic, I soaked in this moment of utter bliss, and I allowed myself to be drenched in the peace. This was an act of love. This was how I wanted to feel.

This was what raising my standards looked like.

In the weeks that followed, I became ruthlessly obsessed with being curious about where my standards were. I'd play games and ask myself questions and be completely open to the possibility that my standards were in total alignment with the highest, best, and most authentic version of who I was at my core. I made it playful and fun. I asked myself, "Is this action in alignment with the highest, best, and most authentic version of who I am?"

If not, I started to self-inquire. I started to wonder why. Transformation is all about aligning our words with our actions. If you want to change for the better, but all of your actions and behaviours are headed in the opposite direction of where you want to be, you need to put yourself in the corner and ask yourself where the discrepancy lies. This is not about self-bashing and calling yourself out for being a total moron. Transformation from a place of hate never did anyone any good. This process is all about honouring yourself by asking yourself powerful questions that yield powerful answers and powerful results.

Our brains are fascinating things. They can drive us to the darkest edges of our emotions, and they can allow us to experience life through the lens of happiness. You are the creator of that reality. You decide in advance which way you're headed. As soon as you decide, your mind is like a dog with a bone and fetches evidence as to why what you've decided is true.

The best part of this is the subconscious doesn't know the difference between fact and fiction. It really has no idea if something has actually happened or not. This is where the game gets fun. We can essentially rewire our minds with new standards – a new way of living that is conducive to how we want to live and how we want to feel.

This is where the magic is. This process is about visceral feelings and visualizing the reality you want to create. When the reality is so clear you can feel it, it's your responsibility to anchor in that reality daily to let your mind know what is up. If that image and reality isn't created clearly enough, the mind will default back to the old program and belief that it knows best.

I'm going to bust a fear that I know is coming up for you. How do I know? Because this is a fear that runs deep within the majority of my clients. This is a fear that is no one talks about openly, but when I talk about it at one of my retreats or live events, nearly everyone in the room raises their hand. "But Sam, if I act as if I'm already there, I feel like a fraud."

I get it, girl. Oh yes, I get all of it. And there is the thing – this whole "feeling like a fraud" thing isn't exclusive to just this area of your life. I know it is showing up in most areas of your life. How do I know? Because if you're reading this book, and you've gotten this far, you're a lot like me.

I feel you. The fear of being a fraud is a common fear that needs to be talked about and healed. If not, it will continue to dig its fangs into our souls and stop us from taking action on becoming higher versions of ourselves. Anytime we break the mold of what people expect us to be, we are losing a part of an identity we've spent years creating, even if that particular identity isn't reflective of who we really are. So we continue to play these roles and wear these masks to keep everyone and their dog around us happy.

When I first started my business, I felt like I was walking around with a "fraud" sign on my forehead. Who was I to lead a movement to help women overcome their battles with food and their bodies? I've literally just ended the darkest days of my life. Who is going to listen to me? My self-doubt was debilitating, and that fear almost keep me stuck in my story and the whole Hungry for Happiness world would be non-existent. I had to check myself in a big way.

One of my dear mentors said to me, "Get over yourself. There are people waiting for you." That one sentence slapped me in the face.

Shit, I thought. This isn't about me at all, this is about the world.

It was essential that I shift the story of "I'm a fraud" into something that was conducive to where I wanted to go. The fear of being a fraud was my ego trying to keep me safe and small. It was there to protect me, and for that, I had to honour it and love it, but choose to not give into the grip it had on me. This was all learning. This is what it look for me to shed the layer.

I know this is starting to resonate with you. Whether it's a business, a role you're playing in your life, or a job, whatever it might be, you have a belief that you're a fraud or not good enough to pursue that particular thing. Take ownership of the thought and commit to shifting it now. It simply comes down to a decisive decision.

I knew I needed to raise my standards, get out of my own way, and show up in the world in a way that was good for my soul. This is simply a choice that doesn't need evidence in order for it to happen. Stop wanting it, and start creating it.

Give yourself the gift of inspired action, rather than forced action. Dieting is a great example of forced action: taking action out of fear, hating your body, and simply denying what is. You know this doesn't work. Decide now that you are not going to wait until things become too much to bear before you create change in your life. That way of operating is old school.

We are constantly told that transformation through fear is the only way we can change. The weight loss industry tells us this all the time in the wonderful world of marketing. They play to your insecurities so you throw money down on a product that is apparently going to fix the problem you think you have. Choose not to be a victim – choose to rise above. Dismiss the excuses as to why you aren't worthy of what you want. Your excuses are not indicative of reality, nor are they productive in the journey to raising your standards.

We can't manipulate our behaviour and expect sustainable transformation. That will only work for a little while, until we can't bear the resistance and we go back to what we have always done. When you diet, what you're really searching for is a feeling. What you really want is the feeling of lightness, contentment, ease, and peace. And what do you do? You measure and manage every calorie that passes through your mouth in an attempt to lose the weight in hopes of feeling content when you see the magic number on the scale. That is, until you decide that your obsession is creating too much havoc on your life and you revert to the shame of filling your emotions with food.

Beliefs create thoughts, thoughts create feelings, feelings create actions, and actions create results. Read that one more time, and let it sink in.

Stop changing the behaviour and expecting your life to flip on its head to achieve the life you want. Start at the belief level and allow the work of shifting internally begin to change your actions and results.

I know you're probably reading this thinking, "Sam, for God sakes! I just want to lose this weight." I get it. I really do.

I support lightness, and I believe if you want to go through your human experience on a lighter frame, all the power to you, girl. You decide what you want. You're worthy and deserving of exactly what you want. But, here is the kicker. You must go about it in the right way. Shaming your way skinny isn't going to work. You can end your suffering as soon as you decide to end the battle of staying stuck in your story. Transformation starts with mental shifts, not behavioral ones.

At first, raising my standards was one of the hardest things for me to do. My mind was being a rebellious hooligan that wouldn't fucking sit still. I had kind of half-decided I was going to raise my standards. I remember sitting on the balcony of my apartment, finishing a chai tea latte, and getting ready to head to a women's circle. I had my feet up on the railing, and I was observing the thoughts in my mind. If I had spoken these thoughts out loud, someone would have checked me into a mental hospital. It was awful. You know when you listen to a two-year-old have a complete shit fit in the grocery store? That was basically what was happening in my mind, except I wasn't complaining that I couldn't have a candy bar. My mind was rattling off words of intense self-sabotage and self-hatred.

"You're never going to change."
"You'll be stuck fighting food for the rest of your life."
"What is the point?"
"You think you have the inner power? HA! Yeah, right!"

All sorts of harmful comments were flooding my psyche, making me want to take my ceramic mug and shove it right in my face. The pain of the impact would be easier to handle then the pain of the thoughts. I dumped the rest of the cold latte in the sink, put my on Ugg boots, and dragged myself to the circle. It was the first time in a long time that I came to face the obvious difference between how I was showing up for myself and what was really going on in my mind. I sat in the circle and shared with the group how far I'd come and how good it felt.

Lies. All fucking lies. I was a fraud, and it sucked the life out of me. Here I was at this circle, where were supposed to be open and honest and I was blatantly lying to the other women, telling them how good everything was going in my inner world. I didn't want to be perceived as weak or unworthy, so I stayed comfortably in my own vortex of denial.

I went home that night and had a fistfight with my pillow. I was so angry at myself. I was angry I was fighting food, I was angry I hated my body, and I was angry at the world. I ugly cried for hours that night, screaming out "Why?" repeatedly, until my lungs were felt like they were bleeding. I smashed pillows, tore paper, and ripped clothes off hangers. I threw down every ounce of anger I had. I'm surprised one of my neighbours didn't call the police with a noise complaint.

I woke up the next morning with puffy eyes and a lighter heart. I crawled out of bed and stood on my balcony.

I felt the crisp air dance on my face, and I noticed colours and beauty I'd never seen in the twelve months I'd been back in Vancouver.

What just happened? I wondered as I stared out. Why do I feel different? What happened to my mind chatter?
People talk about spiritual awakenings. This definitely wasn't one of those, but the world looked clearer, more beautiful, and calmer.

I shut my door, put in my headphones, and sat in meditation for 20 minutes. I focused on the word "clarity." I sat there and observed my thoughts, which weren't running me over like a steam roller for once. I felt grateful for the peace, so I felt into it more. At about the 15-minute mark, I had a clear message. Many people talk about being sent messages in meditation, and I had always thought this was a load of garbage, until now.

It was a gentle whisper: You're safe to fly.

This whisper kept repeating itself, and each time it did, my soul calmed down more and more until I felt I was in a meditative trance. Even if I wanted to move, I don't think it would have been possible.

In that meditation, I was finally given permission to love the negative thoughts, permission not to believe them, permission to own my power, and permission to raise my standards. I felt the release of emotion, and the tears were uncontrollable. It was as if all the trapped emotion I was hiding with strong words of denial were landing on my lap. I didn't fight them. I needed this more than I knew. For once, I didn't apologize for my tears and emotional release – I just let it happen.

After I came out of meditation, I lay down on the floor and let myself breathe. I could feel the cold floor under my heated body. My mind was silent, and I felt peace. It felt like I was breathing for the first time, as if I had been faking even my breathing for most of my life. I didn't want to move, not because I couldn't, but because I was in total awe and fascination of the feeling I was experiencing.

After what felt like hours, I lifted myself off the floor, sauntered into the kitchen, and poured myself a glass of water. I was noticing everything: the floor under my feet, the smell of the vanilla scented air freshener, the coolness of air in the room. Everything felt tangible. I took a massive swig of water and I felt the journey of that cold water through my body. I was feeling all the sensations in my body, both physical and emotional.

I am safe to feel, I thought to myself, as I was in a total state of observation. For years of my life, I didn't think I was safe to feel my emotions, mostly because I didn't trust I would be able to handle them.

During my time in the kitchen, I felt love. It was self-love, not manufactured love. This was different – this was unconditional. I was there, with myself, in my body, simply loving it. In this state, there was no hate, no urge to perform acts of self-violence with food – the thought of body shaming wasn't even an option, because I felt such a powerful connection to my body. The moment felt pure, uninterrupted by fear and the need to change my body, and I knew I was no longer a fraud. I was worthy and could raise my standards to accept only beliefs that were in alignment with the highest, best, and most authentic version of myself.

This was beautiful.
Life was beautiful.
I was beautiful.

PRACTICE IN ACTION

Think about this for a moment: How are you supposed to create change in your life if you've not yet raised your personal standards of excellence? This is why dieting doesn't work. You are still operating under your old standards of who you used to be. You're trying to change your behaviors before you change your beliefs.

I promise you that this will fail you each and every time. Sustainable long term change happens when we are ruthlessly committed to it. It doesn't happen when we dip our toes in or take action from a place of "let's see if this works." You have to decide you're worth it. If you've not made that decision, you are not going to change. You will find yourself saying, "Fuck it!" and bingeing on the hidden stash of chocolate you have in your secret drawer.

It's time to get real with yourself. It's time to evaluate where are you are at, what you want, and how bad you want it.

EXERCISE #9

Complete this writing exercise while being as honest as possible with yourself.

You say you want to create change, but are you willing to get uncomfortable in order to create it?

We fail when there is a difference between our standards and our actions. Currently, where are your standards for your life? How committed are you to excellence?

Describe what your life is going to look like when you're operating from the highest, best, and most authentic version of yourself.

For extra accountability, share your answers with the tribe. When we voice the things we feel shame about, we are committing to change. We've already begun the process of inner transformation.

MANTRA

Personal excellence is my birthright.

THE DEATH OF DIETING
Chapter 10

When we consider the causes of being overweight, we realize the weight was manufactured in fear. When we overeat, we are being violent towards ourselves, harming the beautiful, whole and perfect thing that is our bodies. Dieting throws us into a state of fear-based consumption that comes from a negative emotional trigger from our day or a fear that has been present in our souls for the majority of our lives.

Dieting is rooted in fear. We are running away from our bodies, hating them, shaming them and looking for the best quick fix to alter the current size and shape of our bodies. Every day, we are subjected to the marketing campaigns of the multi-billion dollar weight loss industry, which tell us that there is still more work to do on our bodies, because we've not quite "made it" yet. They paint these beautiful images of what we could have if only we ate a little less and worked out a little more.

Albert Einstein once said, "We cannot solve our problems with the same thinking we used when we created them." Our society is programmed to believe dieting is the answer for weight loss. Dieting and binge eating are rooted in fear. You're trying to numb something, cover it up, and push it down. Therefore, there is no way that fear is going to heal the part of us we don't like. We need to love. Only love will alkalize the fear and allow us to heal. Fear disconnects us, keeps us up in our heads. Fear is why we over-analyze and obsess over calories and exercise. When we are counting calories, or weighing food portions, or feel guilty for overeating 100 calories over what we "should" have eaten that day, it's all fear.

Now I know what you're thinking: "But Sam, if I love myself, then I will never lose weight! I will become a complacent fat lump sitting on my couch all day just loving myself." If your fear wasn't word-for-word in line with that, I'm sure it was something close to that. Acceptance is not synonymous with complacency.

Acceptance will set you free. Acceptance will allow you to feel peace. Acceptance will clear all that mental chatter that has been clogging your brain and causes you to think horrible thoughts and do horrible things. Acceptance creates ease, and it allow us to see what is, for what it is, right in the moment. Acceptance does not distort our current view of what is yet, it allows us to connect with the present moment, being real, being raw, and being secure with all that we are, no matter our size.

Acceptance does not mean you are going to stay stuck. This is where your ego likes to come in and fuck everything up. It doesn't mean you are going to accept yourself and stay at your current weight. Acceptance means you are finally ready to welcome peace and ease and allow that to be the baseline of your transformation. Give yourself permission to allow it to be easy. Yes, you can allow yourself to transform through ease.

Humans are fundamentally designed for ease and happiness; however, this is what the weight loss industry doesn't want to tell us. They want to keep playing on your insecurities, keeping you stuck in fear, keeping you thinking that you need to find something in order to transform. There is nothing to find or discover. There is nothing you are doing wrong. You are perfect and whole. You have all the answers, power, and guidance you need to completely transform your body and your mind. I want you to come to a place where you don't need this book, you don't need me, my work or my retreats. I want you to come to a place where you feel full, perfect, and complete.
This is the place you were designed to be: a place where everything you need to heal whatever pain arises in your body is within you now.

There is nothing you need to consume or acquire, because you have it already.

You need to feel it, because when you feel it, it will become useful and transformational. I wish for all humans to reach a place where they are fully embodied in this truth, where they have access to their higher self to guide them. No one on this earth is exempt from this truth. It's within us all. Whether or not we chose to believe it, embody it, and use it is completely up to us.

While running a retreat in Bali, I was working with a client named Julie, and during one of the sessions, I was coaching her on the importance of having gratitude for your body. I said to her, "Julie, what you appreciate, appreciates."

She looked at me with puzzled eyes and said with a straight face, "So, if I appreciate my body, I will get fatter?"

I had to laugh at the irony of this comment, but when I thought about it more, I realized this is what many woman believe when they think about loving their body as it is. They assume they will just be a 300 pound woman, bedridden, with 20 cats, and no friends. When we come to realize this thought pattern is simply the fear we have, we can finally feel free knowing that we are free to love ourselves at the weight we are at.

Transformation at the deepest level happens when we accept the present while creating the future. No running, no hiding, no shaming – just loving. The journey to true transformation is so much more beautiful, peaceful, and easy. Remember, you weren't designed to struggle. Struggle is a learned behaviour.

It's important to note here that our intentions need to be stronger than our desire to have it all planned out. Our ego loves a plan, a linear step-by-step system to achieve what it is we think we want to achieve. We are always looking for the "how" and ignoring the "why." Connecting with to the vision of our higher selves with clarity and certainty allows it to be created in the mind first. Everything in the world is created twice: once in the mind and once in the material world. Fully embody the essence of what you desire, now – before you have it. Feel the emotions first, and allow yourself to melt into the feeling of lightness before you achieve it. Act as if you're already there. Intention must proceed progress. When your intention is clear, obstacles disappear.

When we are solely focused on manipulating our behaviours to change our bodies, we've not communicated with our higher selves where we are going and why we are doing it. We are operating from fear and ego, and from this place we have no access to our power source: our intuitive guidance.

Dieting is a good idea until the shame of failing percolates through your pores. Dieting is a good idea until you turn into a head case, ignoring people around you and sitting on your hands to avoid devouring the plate of brownies. Dieting is a good idea until you realize that you're ruining your life, saying no to social engagements while you sit at home sipping shit tea and wondering how many calories you've consumed that day. Dieting is a good idea until you wake up and realize that it's not the physical weight that is the problem, it's the emotional weight.

You're dieting because you hate your body — let's just make that clear. You can look in the mirror and convince yourself that you're dieting "for health reasons," but when you're starving yourself and jumping on and off the scale multiple times a day, you're not kidding anyone.

At one point in my journey, I started seeing an intuitive healer. A few months before, I would have thought seeing an intuitive healer was too "woo woo," but I had been through a lot, and I figured anything was worth a shot at this point.

Maria was a spiritual powerhouse that was always willing to give me a spiritual slap in the face whenever I needed one. During one of our sessions, she said something to me that was one of the most profound insights I could have received. At first this insight terrified me to my core, and I wanted to run out of her office and end the whole journey, but I was too far along, too far emotionally, mentally, spiritually, and physically invested.

Maria leaned in, touched my leg, and said to me in her soft South African accent, "Darling, in order to heal, you have to be okay with getting fat."

I nearly spat my tea all over her beautiful velvet couch. For a moment I thought she was joking, or that I misunderstood her. My blood pressure increased and my throat began to close.

"Umm, excuse me?" I said to her, looking at her as if I'd seen a ghost.

"You're still way too attached to the number on the scale. You're run by it. Fear is still the driving force in your recovery. You are making incredible progress with intuition and tapping into your soul, yet you are limited by the fear of gaining weight. You're not trusting yourself at the level you need to in order to fully overcome this. Until you do, you'll still be fighting yourself, tripping over the obstacles, trying to find your way. Until the number on the scale doesn't represent your worth, you'll be stuck."

Her words ripped through me like a freight train speeding through a sleepy town in the middle of the night. I tried to digest what has just happened. I knew this is what I needed to hear, but my higher self was giving Maria a high five while my ego wanted to punch her right in the face.

After our session, I tried to visualize what life would be like if I was 200 pounds heavier. My ego took this for a ride, and I played out all of the worst-case-scenarios in my mind during that fifteen minute walk back home. For God's sake, Samantha. Stop being such a drama queen.

I was being called to rise. I was being called to up level, to fully release the fear in my body, and trust in my higher self. I had an opportunity to connect deeper into my body, listen to it with more love, and honour it with more grace. This process was all by divine design: releasing my attachment to the number on the scale was my access point to healing my body. This felt like the final obstacle keeping me at arm's length from fully healing.

I spent the next week repeating a mantra in my head: "I am safe to trust my body. My body is safe to trust me." I knew if I was completely in tune with my body and honouring its emotional and physical hunger cues from a place of acceptance and love, I couldn't fail, I was supported by something much bigger than myself. I wasn't searching for a size, I was searching for a feeling – the feeling of being light: lightness in mind and lightness in my heart. Lightness didn't come as a number value, and it wasn't the result of doing the latest fad diet.

Lightness was a feeling I chose and I could deepen the feeling of lightness whenever I decided to. This feeling was not manufactured in dieting, in fact, dieting only distanced me from having access to this feeling. Settling into love, allowing myself to experience inner peace in my body and lightness in my mind created the conditions to transform and move through the pain of my recovery.

It's important to note that when we are transforming our minds and bodies, we are releasing, we aren't losing. What happens when you lose your keys? You race around the house in a frenzy trying to find them, and you finally do. You lose, you find.

When it comes to our bodies, we don't want to lose weight, we want to release it. We want to release the emotional weight so that we can release the physical weight. I needed to fully release the belief that my weight was congruent with my worth, and releasing this belief cleared up my emotional landscape to invite beliefs in that were in total alignment with the woman I knew I was destined to become.

Love and acceptance is present when we look at what is, without the impulse to run from it, avoid it, or change it. It's a matter of taking full ownership: looking in a mirror completely naked and loving every piece of yourself. I know as you consider this idea, there are all sorts of things that come up for you. There is resistance, fear, and disgust, especially if you usually try to do whatever it takes to avoid mirrors at all costs. I promise you will get to a point where you can look at your body, no matter what size it is, and have a profound love and appreciation for it – to look at the "flaws" and "imperfections" and just be in awe of the masterpiece that is in front of you. You are not only the creator of your world, but you are also the creator of your body. What you see in the mirror is a reflection of your beliefs and your standards. It's a reflection of your deeply rooted beliefs about who you are. Your body is providing you with so much information. Every fat cell on your body is communicating a story to you – a story of your life, your path, and your decisions. Does the story bring you joy, or does it fill you with pain? There is no right or wrong, good or bad. It's simply just information. When we can be at peace with this information while having strong intentions of how we want to use the information to transform ourselves, we will find freedom and liberation.

As beautiful and powerful as your mind is, it's not strong enough to break you out of the battle you're experiencing with food and your body on its own. You're reading this book because you've given up on trying. You've given up on doing all the hard work. You are craving peace and contentment. The journey back into your body and listening to the subtle call of your soul requires you to allow your body to be guided from within. You finally get to listen to what your body really wants at a fundamental level. You get to experience the joy of being integral to what it needs in each moment.

Committing to stop dieting takes a decisive decision. It also requires a high element of forgiveness. Apologizing to your body for treating it so poorly, disowning it, starving it, overfeeding it and abusing it. Your body has never disowned you. It's always had your back. It's time to clear the energy that has created an intense amount of animosity between your mind and body. Forgive yourself for acting the way you did and treating your body the way you have.

Maybe you knew better, but you didn't know how to shift these patterns. Now you are learning, and it's time to clear all the broken trust and broken agreements and start fresh. Your body is waiting for this – it's waiting to be loved, waiting to be trusted, and waiting for the harmonious union to take place where your mind and body are communicating and connected.

Forgiving ourselves for dieting obsessively is critical. So is forgiveness for allowing our minds to bully us into destructive behaviours. We have to forgive the part of us that thought it was a good idea to shame-our-way-skinny, the part of us that thought hating ourselves into a place of peace would work. You are free to fully release all of this pain, and it's your divine responsibility to no longer be defined by your past actions. Just as the sun rises each morning, you are free to rise, free to decide differently, free to commit to living in alignment with your higher self.

Expand your capacity to forgive yourself beyond just your issues with food, and allow yourself to explore all the areas of your life where you haven't been your highest self – areas where you've done something because you wanted to feel loved, appreciated, or heard. Don't just think about the recent past when you are doing your forgiveness work, extend it back as far as you need to go. This process is called timeline forgiveness. Think about yourself a child: when did you first feel guilty or shameful for something you did? That energy is still locked inside your body as pockets of unhealed shame that is causing animosity within your body. It's time to release this pain, transform it into compassion, and create a solid foundation going forward.

This work requires you to clean your proverbial slate. A solid foundation of strength is required when we are doing this work. When we commit ourselves to growth, we are committing ourselves to "going through the shit." It can be easy to be knocked off course and throw in the towel if we don't start from a powerful place of acceptance, love, and compassion. Spend time with your past self, fully forgiving yourself and releasing any resentment you hold. You owe it to yourself to clear those energetic drains and channel your energy into becoming the highest, best, and most authentic version of yourself.

PRACTICE IN ACTION

What is the core reason why we diet? We want to feel differently. You're not searching for a size, you're searching for a feeling. For many of the women I work with, that feeling is freedom, peace, ease, happiness, or lightness. You assume being at a certain weight will allow you to feel that desired feeling. It's essential we start with that feeling: become the feeling, allow ourselves to feel it now, not to delay our happiness and prolong our suffering.

We use food (restrict it and overeat it) to avoid feeling. When we don't honour our body's intuitive calls, we are acting from a place of self-violence, and we don't honour and heal the pain we have trapped in our bodies.

Your time to heal is now.

EXERCISE #10

Take some time to reflect on and answer the questions below.

What is the feeling I want to feel?
What am I afraid of feeling?
What is it costing me not to feel my feelings?
What is it costing me to stay stuck in the diet/binge cycle?

We learned in this chapter that physical weight is a representation of emotional weight. Every pound represents a difficult conversation we aren't willing to have, a fear we aren't willing to overcome, or a childhood wound we don't want to heal. It's all starts on our emotional landscape. Now, I want you to start to explore what that emotional weight might be for you. Note that if you are a restrictor when it comes to food and your body, this exercise still applies. Each time you choose to restrict, what are you not willing to face and to feel?

Spend some time and explore your inner state. This requires you to feel. In order to heal we must be willing to feel. So often when clients come to me and I ask them to explore their childhood, they will say they have no memory of it. This isn't really the case. They've just subconsciously chosen to not let themselves remember and feel the emotions linked to the memory. They've put up a wall, and they're guarding themselves from truly feeling. Once you give yourself permission to remember, feel the emotion, and heal, you will unlock years of memory. This is a beautiful process, because when we have data on what needs to be healed, we can begin to love it. Without this awareness, we have no room to explore.

I want you to complete the sentence below, thinking of as many things as possible to fill the blank. This may take more than one sitting; in fact, most of my clients do this multiple times. Be patient with the exercise, and allow the words to come to you. Do not chase them. Remember, your body will not give you anything you can't handle.

Finish the following sentence as many times as you need to

"Having awareness and love around _____
allows me to fully feel it, and therefore heal it."

MANTRA

I fully allow myself to feel and heal all I've been resisting.

YOUR BODY KNOWS BEST
Chapter 11

The resistance you're feeling, the disconnection in your mind, in your heart, and in your soul, is largely because you simply don't trust yourself. You assume you don't have the answers. You assume everyone and their dog knows what's best for you or what the hell you should do with your life. You are giving away your power like Halloween candy. You can get all the advice in the world, but you still feel fearful when making a decision.

And before you toss yourself into a pool of self-sabotage, I want to remind you of something critical: this is all learned behaviour. You learned how to struggle; you learned how to question your intuition. Think about yourself as a child. You would toss yourself into situations, throw caution to the wind, give it your all, and never stop to think, "I don't trust myself." You just powered ahead with your soul, trusting that fire you felt in your body, trusting it was the right thing to do. Where along the way did you lose this? Why is it like trying to find a damn needle in a hack stack to find a little bit of trust within our hearts?

Here is the good news, my friend: that trust is there. It always has been, and it always will be. What's blocking the trust are the stories you've created about why you're not trustworthy.

Here is the deal, when we think about making a move in our lives that require us to trust ourselves, our minds automatically take an inventory of the amount of trust we have stored up in our bodies. For most of us, that inventory comes back as zilch, and we find it incredibly difficult to take action. We base the amount of trust we have towards our bodies on circumstances or events that have taken place in the past. When we diet, we are basically saying to our bodies, "I don't trust you. I am going to take over and do it my way." So, we hop on the latest restrictive diet that eventually digs us into the ever-familiar place of failure. We fail the diet, we fail ourselves, we fail at life – this is the conclusion we come to in our minds. Because this isn't the first time we've tried and failed at a diet, these behaviours just add leverage to the story of "I don't trust myself."

You buy all the good food, you write down all the calories, and you carefully map out your week, ensuring you eliminate anything that would cause you to fuck it all up. And when you inevitably do fail at dieting, you chalk it up to the fact you have no willpower or are a total failure. You've been working really hard at developing this story, and you have a lot of evidence to support the story already, perhaps 20 years' worth of evidence as to why you aren't trustworthy. When you take action with this story in mind, you're already on the path to destruction and failure. Fundamentally, you don't believe you're going to "win" at dieting, so when you fail, there is a small part of you that is satisfied in knowing your actions are congruent with the story you've created in your mind.

Think of a friend you have who has let you down repeatedly. She's canceled plans, told others your secrets, and lied to your face. You know the kind of friend I'm talking about, and I use the term "friend" loosely here. Hopefully, by now, you've reduced her to just strictly a Facebook friend, if anything at all. But, the question is, do you trust this person? The answer is of course, absolutely not! You've completely lost all trust in her, you've written her off, and decided she doesn't deserve a place in your life. Fair enough.

Now, what you must realize is, you are just like that lie-telling-plan-cancelling girl who you don't trust. You are breaking trust agreements with yourself every time you diet. When you say you're going to do something but don't follow through, you break an agreement. When you diet, you break an agreement. You've had a history of breaking agreements you've made, which is leaving on you on very shaky ground as far as trusting yourself goes.

When you commit and decide to rebuild the trust you have with yourself, you mustn't test the part of you – your ego – that has let you down time and time again. You need to trust your soul – the deeper part of you – the intersection of the mind and body, the calm, knowing, confident place in you that is fully capable and willing to support you in any decision you make, whether that decision is with food, your body, relationships, money, or sex. This part of you has been stifled in your attempts to change your body during your dieting career. There is no room for it to breathe and co-exist with the noise of your mind and the fear you have around food and your body. When that little voice is telling you to try just one more diet, you are ignoring the inner guidance you have waiting to be released. Your soul is begging for you to trust it. Your soul is intuitive and knows exactly what you need.

But you're terrified. You're terrified of getting fat, terrified of eating down the house, and all the worst-case scenarios run through your mind keeping you stuck in the cycle. You'll stay stuck and stagnant until you realize you have the power to end the battle. There is an untapped, unlimited source of self-trust lying dormant in your body. Its power is wasting away in your body. It will continue to waste away until you tap into it and use it to support you in becoming the highest, best, and most authentic version of yourself. You were designed to use its unlimited ability to guide you. Only you and your fear are blocking the brilliance of your inner world.

Humans are funny creatures. When we step back and look at the things we do to feel a certain way, it's comedy gold. We try and manipulate our environments, things we come in contact with, things we consume, and we try and change bloody everything except our beliefs – the one thing that actually works in changing our lives. The quality of our lives is a direct result of the beliefs we have about ourselves.

Our feelings are a manifestation of the thoughts we have on a daily basis. When these thoughts are circling around in our brains, they create certain feelings in our bodies. "I am not worthy" creates a much different reaction in your body than "I am perfect and whole." You know the difference I am talking about. In fact, do that right now. Say both sentences aloud, and feel them fully. Feel the visceral difference in your body.

Our behaviors are directly linked to how we are feeling. When we are vibrating at a higher level, we take action out of love, and we do things that are aligned with our higher self. When we are vibrating at a lower level with shame and guilt, our actions are rooted in fear.

Our core beliefs create these thoughts in our minds. If we can have awareness around the thoughts we are thinking, we can trace them back and identity what core belief about ourselves has perpetuated this thought. We then have the awareness to shift this belief at our core. But here is where we get hung up: we get too busy trying to changing our behaviours, manipulating our experience so that we lose sight of where the real issue is. The lack of trust is deeply rooted in your system. It's a story you've adapted and reinforced for years, so letting go of it will seem like there is a piece of you dying, which there is, but it's a piece of you that never needed to be there in the first place. Allow the death to happen with ease. Allow the part of you that thinks you are untrustworthy to fade away as you reawaken the trust within you – the trust that your body knows what it needs.

For the majority of my life, I was completely disconnected from my body. I barely trusted it to take my next breath. A simple trip to the ice cream shop would be a stressful ordeal. I would be sweating in the ice cream shop wondering if my entire life would be affected if I decided to go with Tiger Stripe over Bubble Gum ice cream. I'm telling you, the struggle was real. But in all seriousness, each time I was faced with a difficult decision, I would ask around, text my friends, finally make a decision, and then doubt my decision for weeks to come. It was an exhausting process.

When I first starting exploring this whole intuition thing, I was completely thrown off. For months on end, I convinced my therapist (and myself) that my intuition wanted the whole row of Oreos. I would plead my case with such conviction that my therapist just stared back at me in silence, likely thinking that I was on a day pass from the mental hospital. He then said something to me that I've never considered in my entire career of disordered eating: "Darling, that isn't your intuition. That is your mind. Your mind is convincing you that you need those Oreos or else you'll die."

It was an interesting realization. I could have convinced anyone that my body and my intuition were dying for that chocolatey goodness. After that session, I realized that the guidance of my body is much different from my mind, and one of the most important things I can do is properly identify the difference. While working through the struggle I had with food and my body, I would often dismiss the work of identifying the difference between messages from my body and my mind as useless or "woo woo," because it didn't fit within my logical mind. If I couldn't see it or feel it with my own two hands, it didn't exist.

I laughed at a lot of the homework my therapist gave me and had zero intentions of actually doing it, which of course prolonged my suffering until I got over myself, and used the advice for which I was paying thousands of dollars.

"You need to figure out the difference between an intuitive body 'yes' and 'no' versus a 'yes' or 'no' that is driven by the mind."

My homework was to figure out the difference between a mind yes and no, and a body yes and no. This was mind-blowing to me. I had to be in the presence of food, ask myself if that was what I really was hungry for, and then observe the reaction in my body.

For the next few weeks, I was ruthlessly committed to finding the underlying cause of this, as I had a strong hunch this would be the access point to having more awareness in my body and making more intuitive decisions around food. When I let my mind control my behavior, I would get into almost a state of hypnosis where I literally cut off access to my body and my mind ran the show. Once I started to try to negotiate with my mind, the game was over. My mind would always win.

The voice of the ego and the mind is much louder than the gentle whisper of the intuition. Accessing this part of my body was impossible without being present. It was essential that I be fully in the present moment before I could access this part of my body. By virtue of asking my body these questions, my body immediately brought me into the present moment, and I was able to transition from fighting with my mind to simply observing my mind.

I made this exercise fun and playful. When we are in a state of playing or have an element of fun attached to learning and exploring, it's easier to learn. One of my top values is fun, and something I say frequently is "If it's not fun, I'm not doing it." Allowing myself to have fun with this exploration turned it into a pleasure rather than a burden. Adding an element of fun, mixed with curiosity and compassion, allowed me to be gentle with myself and let go of my perfectionism.

We can't build trust without taking action. We must push our boundaries, take action, and explore what letting go and trusting truly feels like. In order not to freak out our ego, it's essential we start small, with seemingly insignificant decisions. Surrender the mind, and allow your body to guide the decision. Ask your body the question, and notice the message and inner guidance it's trying communicate.

Remember, presence is key with this exercise: use presence and your breath to ground yourself. Connection to the body always enhances communication with the soul. Anger, frustration, and fear block the flow of information from our intuition. Here is the deal: you need to give up your addiction to having everything be a struggle.

You need to go with what feels right and avoid negotiating with the mind. Follow the first hunch you have, fully commit to it, and don't give into the temptation of the grass-is-greener-syndrome. If you encounter pain or resistance to the decision you've made, your mind will label it as the "wrong" decision, and this is simply the mind at play making a decision on the current evidence and not looking at the bigger picture.

When we are faced with adversity, it's an opportunity for growth. When things aren't easy, we are invited to rise and cultivate the strength we need to move through the pain and come out stronger. This is where we miss the mark. In situations where something does not come to us easily, we label it as a wrong move, shame ourselves, and fail to look for an opportunity for growth. Provided you are following your intuition and doing what feels right, there are no wrong moves.

Every action you take leads you to victory or growth. It's not up to you to decide if it's good or bad. Life is happening for you, not to you. Read that last sentence again and let it marinate.

Life is happening for you, not to you. Your life is being created by divine design, so there are no mistakes or coincidences, only intuition to guide you along the path, allowing you to experience more of your truth and ultimately walk you home to your soul.

Sometimes I felt like my therapist was just trying to make me crazy, but perception is everything, and when we see others as teachers (and not assholes) and we see an opportunity for growth rather than struggle. We are able to be in a place of ultimate appreciation. When we shift our perception to view the world this way, life becomes a game of growth, expansion, and play. It's game that is unfolding perfectly for you, in each and every moment.

Trusting the timing of your life events is also an important piece to note here. When learning how to trust themselves, a lot of my clients are living in a place of time scarcity, thinking they are running out of time to complete all the things they want to do in their lives.

"When am I going to get laid, and when am I going to get paid?" That's the question a lot of the younger women I work with ask; they want a partner, and they want a financial success. NOW. Sex and money hold a lot of energy, and we have to surrender and trust both are happening by divine design, which allows us to stay present in our experience.

Feeling inadequate for not being in a committed relationship in the timeframe you created when you were 15 denies you the reality of what is, and if you are in denial of what is, you are at war with yourself.

In this place of denial, you "should" all over yourself..."I should be married by now"..."I should be making X amount of money by now." You shame yourself because you haven't yet hit the mark of where you thought you "should" have been by now. This energy will retract you even more from where you think you want to be. Invite in appreciation and acceptance of what is. Settle into the profound knowing that everything is working out for you in perfect timing.

During my diet depression, my life would always be a massive race to the finish line, except there was no finish line – there was no line at all. I was a hamster on a wheel, always reaching for the next thing, but never really getting anywhere. My life was rushed and chaotic, fogged by noise from my mind and manufactured distraction. I lost touch with the essence of just being – savouring each moment, allowing myself to be present, and appreciate the gifts I had in the present moment. I overlooked these gifts; I cock-blocked miracles by being distracted, rushed, and fearful. I rushed through meals, exercise, work, my career – always trying to get there, wherever "there" was. I was terrified I'd fall behind if I allowed myself to slow down., I was terrified I'd gain weight, not be perfect or I'd disappoint my parents by not being farther ahead in life.

There are magic moments and miracles in every single moment of your life. Stop reading this book for a moment, and look around the room you're in. Notice the colours, notice the beauty, notice your breath, notice how you feel. Savour the moment. A series of beautiful moments needed to occur for you to be sitting here with this book in your hands. You were guided here; it was all by divine design. Settle into this truth and appreciate it. This was not a mistake.

PRACTICE IN ACTION

In this chapter, we explored the importance of trusting ourselves. When we trust ourselves, we have a divine connection to our souls. When we live and create from that place, we are literally unstoppable. It's the birthplace of all divine creation.

Given the fact we have the ability to transform ourselves as soon as we decide we want to, it's important to do that on a solid foundation of trust.

EXERCISE #11

We create inner trust through taking action. Remember; don't try to make everything clear before you take action. It's essential we don't just think about how much we do or do not trust ourselves. We literally need to create a new blueprint in our systems. Right now, your story about trust is "You aren't trustworthy: look at all the diets you failed and mistakes you made. You're just one big failure." At least, that's what it was for me. We create new blueprints of trust through action, which is exactly what you need to do now. Feel into your body and ask yourself a question.

Listen for the answer from your intuition. What is it telling you? Take instant action and commit to doing what your intuition is guiding you to do. This is about following the initial hunch you receive from asking your intuition. Do not negotiate with your mind, even if it's the "wrong" answer. Follow it, commit to it. This is where most of us miss the mark, as we allow our logic mind, which simply doesn't have access to energetic reason, to throw us off the game by staying reasonable. The calls of the soul are not always reasonable or sensible. We all know the voice of these calls. They start as a soft whisper and increase their voice as we continue to ignore them.

"Quit your job."
"Leave your partner."
"Stop dieting."
"Pursue your passion."

This call from the depth of our soul is our call to action – our call to be in deeper alignment with our truth. It excites us, while simultaneously scaring the shit out of us. This is how you know you're in communication with your truth. It's not always easy. The path of following your truth isn't sexy, and it's not always Instagram worthy.

Truth seeking requires you to question the status quo, go against the grain, and be okay with feeling insane in your pursuit to discover yourself. So often, the issue is that we receive the information from our intuition and immediately our mind jumps into negotiation mode to try to rationalize our intuition. Then we come to a standstill and don't make a decision. This exercise is all about making mistakes, taking action, and being progressive. Start small if you must, but you need to "wake up" the system and allow your body to be receptive to the inner guidance your intuition is sending you.

MANTRA

I fully trust my body. My body fully trusts me.

OVERWHELMED AND OVERWEIGHT
Chapter 12

Growing up, I was a hot head. In times of stress, I would lose it, scream bloody murder, and throw things, just to ensure my family understood how angry I was. I must have looked like a crazy child. But, knowing what I know now, it was one of the smartest things I could have done to release my anger. For the record, I continue to scream at the top of my lungs when I'm angry, except I do it alone in my car.

When I feel anger bubbling up, I put myself in the time out and scream until I feel the release in my body. I scream out the weight I've been carrying on my chest, and it's freeing and beautiful.

I recently bought myself a new car, and as I was test-driving it, I turned to the salesperson and asked, "So tell me, exactly how sound proof is this vehicle?"

With a furrow of his brow, he replied, "Very soundproof, you can pump the music super loud and music should stay pretty well contained."

To which I responded, "Oh, it's not for the music, it's for my voice. I like to scream at the top of my lungs when I am angry."

The salesperson slowly turned his face forward, completely confused if I was joking or serious.

Why do we live in a society that frowns upon expression of anger, especially from women? We should never shame our emotions. Anger is an emotion, one that we get to move through and honour. Some of the greatest victories in the world were created out of someone's anger for their current situation, and they decided to use their anger as a catalyst to do something about the issue.

In some way, Hungry for Happiness is the manifestation of the anger I have for the weight loss industry. The anger percolates within me knowing that the weight loss industry is praying on the insecurities of women and men all over the world who are overweight and overwhelmed – the ones who've spent thousands of dollars on the weight loss gimmicks and continue to do so, because they are still convinced that the answers are outside of themselves.

I could just stay angry at an industry that create havoc in my life for so many years. I could easily hide out in my bedroom, behind my computer screen and ridicule the industry though vicious tweets with no intention of taking any productive action. This is how the majority of the world works: we let our anger consume us, rather than releasing it and taking inspired action against the thing that made us angry in the first place.

You're allowed to express your anger through inspired action, and that's a beautiful use of this incredibly powerful emotion. Here is the difference, though: it's about recognizing the anger and the emotion that fires you up and releasing it before you take action. Anger expressed as aggression isn't beneficial or effective for anyone, especially yourself. This process is about taking full responsibility for your anger, acknowledging it, honouring it, processing it, and taking action. Your creation mustn't be rooted in anger, as anger can only be a catalyst for change.

Suppressed anger is one of the main reasons you are using food as a drug. Within your body is powerful energy that is begging to be released, but instead of releasing it, you fear it, you shame it, and you suppress it.

What we resist persists.

When you ignore that energy, it will be powerful, and then you'll turn to food to temporarily numb the emotion that you aren't willing to face or release. On the verge of a binge, the emotion takes over and sends you into a hypnosis-like state. You aren't feeling. You're being controlled by your angry mind. Let's slow this process down.

When anger is in the body, it's a constant residual feeling of pain and disconnection. It's a constant anxiety where your body feels heavy, your mind is foggy, everything is a struggle, and everything is an effort. You may see glimmers of happiness if something external changes your state, but that will last for as long as the external excitement lasts, and you'll be back to your baseline level of stress.

When we decide to use food as a drug, and we are about to go into a binge, we shut off the connection between mind and body, and they operate as two separate units. The mind completely takes over and creates chaotic energy in the body, and if you don't have that half pint of ice cream in the freezer, you will die. That tub of ice cream might as well be the last one on the planet. And you have to eat it. NOW.

When we get in to this state, it's difficult to check ourselves and stop the behaviour. (There's no magical being who is going to smack the ice cream out of your hand.) When we don't take responsibility for our emotions when our body communicates them to us, we allow ourselves to spiral into a late night binge with a hangover of shame and guilt to follow the next day.

What if you knew how to take complete control over your emotions in real time? The body has a wonderful way of letting us know exactly what it needs at any given time, but we have to decide to listen to it. The signs are subtle at first, like a little glimmer in the belly. If we ignore the signs, our body continues to communicate with us more forcefully until we answer its calls. When we choose not to honour our body, it usually winds up smacking us right across the face in the form of a binge.

During my recovery, one of my mentors asked me to take full responsibility for the anger I was feeling in my body. I remember how vulnerable that felt. I couldn't blame anyone or anything else for my anger. I had to own it, deal with it, and heal through it. He went on to say that I had to ensure my anger didn't develop into aggression directed at anyone else.

Hmmm, I thought, so what you're saying is that I can't have impulsive outbursts of aggression because my boyfriend is home late? Ok got it, full responsibility.

First, I had to get real with the emotion in my body, and really acknowledge its presence. Initially, the only thing my mind wanted to do was create meaning around why the anger was there. I did my best to pull up childhood memories as evidence for why the anger was in my body, but this was a waste of time, because it didn't matter. All that mattered was that I knew it was within my body and I needed to release it.

I tried to "self-therapy" myself by thinking of myself as a child. I remember a girl who made up a story that I went to fat camp and got super skinny over one summer. What a bitch. I was so angry that she would say such a thing. Now, in trying to address my feelings about this memory, I wanted to blame my deeply seated anger on her so bad, but again, it didn't matter. I created time and space to allow myself to process the fierce anger I was feeling in my body. First, I journaled about it, how it felt in the present moment, what it was holding me back from, and how heavy it felt to carry around.

Then, I used my physical body to release the anger: I punched, kicked, screamed, and released. If someone had been watching me, they surely would have thought I was on a day pass from a mental hospital. This process is all about being proactive about your emotional landscape and not allowing yourself to be trapped by anger.

We need to love the angry, shadowy parts of ourselves – we are whole because of them, not in spite of them. We are one with them. Hatred or denial of these parts of us will only force us into a fit of external rage or an epic binge. Overeating, which is simply an act of self-hatred, is a last ditch effort to numb the emotion we are feeling in our bodies. The chocolate does a great job of distracting us from the innate pain we are feeling within our souls.

Let's all take a moment and talk about the idea that women who get angry are "crazy bitches", because, yes, it's a thing. Let's all be honest with ourselves.

You freak out at your partner and when the two of you break up because you've freaked out at him one too many times, he tells all his friends that you were a crazy bitch. I'm sure some of us have been there.

The reason why women have impulsive freak-outs is that we haven't expressed our anger to the degree where it can be released in a safe container. You're not crazy because you release anger when you feel it. Although I must admit, screaming in my car down the highway may seem a little odd at times, but it saves me days and sometimes weeks of residual anxiety.

You know that beautiful, cleansing feeling you have after a good cry? The after effects of a good shit fit are very similar. You are safe to express your anger, and it's just as beautiful as expressing your joy. Every emotion we experience is a divine opportunity for us to dig a little deeper into who we are at our core. When we can fully love all parts of ourselves, we have access to growth, enlightenment, and becoming the highest, best, and most authentic versions of who we are. We get the opportunity to become closer to our soul, closer to the truth of who we are. The truth that lies under the stories, the limiting beliefs, the fear, the doubt, and the self-hatred. We have access to it all.

It's time to release the stories you've created in your mind as to why this process isn't available to you — why you don't have access to experiencing release. Anger release comes down to choice. It comes down to making a micro decision when you feel the initial desire to release your anger. And the more you learn to clear this energy from your body in real time, the better you are at mastering your emotions. When you can learn to master your emotions, you can master your life.

As children, we are all taught not to make a scene and be on our best behaviour. We were conditioned not to get angry and to swallow the frustration left percolating in our bodies. We aren't given an outlet to release these emotions in a healthy way. Now as adults, we walk around with an intense amount of suppressed anger, which is manifesting itself as addiction, violence, and self-hatred. We are conditioned to dehumanize ourselves by showing the world the highlight reel of our lives rather than the truth.

We are constantly distancing ourselves from the truth, and therefore our higher selves, which is only perpetuating the cycle of disconnect from our bodies.

Throughout this book, I've had you really examine your life and be raw and honest with yourself. It's been confronting, eye opening, and scary at times. I've asked you to honour, trust, and use your intuition for guidance. It's not just a good idea to follow your intuition, it's a courageous act of self-love that will allow you to live in freedom and liberation.

In order to have clear access to your intuition, we must be mindful of the things that block intuition, anger being one of these blocks. When we are motivated by anger and we are being reactive to its presence in our body, it blocks our truth and fogs our sense of reality. We act out of fear from the power of years of suppressed anger that we are channeling into the current circumstance that is creating tension for us. I'm sure I'm not the only one who has felt shameful for acting out of anger, then regretting it immediately. We all know the feeling the good old "what-the-heck-was-I-thinking?" syndrome.

It's your responsibility to clear your emotional landscape, process your anger, and create space to listen to your body. You must lay strong foundations for this work. Ignored and suppressed anger distances us from clear communication with our intuition. A lot of the time, forgiveness needs to take place in order to clear your emotional landscape, and you have to forgive the people in your life who've done you wrong. Now, let me be clear about something. Forgiveness doesn't make their actions right. However, it allows you to set your anger free.

One of my clients, Karen, had recently gone through a really messy divorce when I started working with her. One day, her husband up and left her, her two daughters, and their dog without warning. Karen was devastated, and her entire life was ripped apart while she was left to fend for herself while supporting her two daughters. Months later when we were working on the forgiveness module in my group-coaching program, Karen said that there was just no way she could ever forgive her ex-husband for what he did.

I asked her what it was going to take her to release the anger and forgive him. She told me that she would go to her grave with the anger and never forgive him for completely uprooting her life and abandoning her. I knew at the time that Karen wasn't in a position to forgive him when the work was first presented. Months later, as the program was wrapping up, she came to me and explained how holding onto her anger was draining her – it was a constant, open loop in her life that consumed her. She told me she was finally ready to cut the cord and release the anger. Karen realized that she needed to forgive her ex-husband, not because she condoned what he did, but because she deserved to forgive and release her anger.

The more cords we have attached to things we are holding onto, the harder it is to find our truth. When we are so consumed with holding grudges and not forgiving ourselves or others we live in a state of resentment, which develops into anger. If you desire a feeling of lightness and peace, you must do the work and release this energy. You owe it to yourself.

PRACTICE IN ACTION

Anger can be a beautiful emotion when it's channeled effectively. The suppression of anger is the root cause of behaviours that are not aligned with the highest versions of ourselves.

It's important not to confuse anger and aggression in this exercise. Anger directed at someone else in a reactive state will land you flat on your ass. This exercise is all about taking personal responsibility for our anger, and giving ourselves permission to process it, so we can effectively clear our emotional landscape.

EXERCISE #12

I am a very vocal person, so when I use my voice to process my anger it feels liberating. When I am at family dinner and I am feeling triggered to the point where I feel it may develop into aggression, I excuse myself, hop in my car, and release the anger by screaming my head off. Then, I call in compassion for whatever made me angry and return to dinner feeling balanced and at ease. Screaming is my thing, but it might not be yours. Find an outlet that feels good to you: punching pillows, running, kickboxing, or whatever. This exercise is about identifying what feels good to you. If one method of releasing anger isn't working for you, try a different method.

I don't want you to manufacture anger as you go through this exercise. What is important is to simply identity what feels right for you and act accordingly. In addition to exploring what method of anger release works best for you, I want you to start exploring the depths of suppressed anger. Allowing yourself to explore any suppressed anger in your body is one of the most beautiful things we can do for ourselves — it's a divine act of self-love. Take some time with your journal to sit down and take inventory anger you hold.

Answer the following questions:

What am I angry with myself for?
What am I angry with others for?
What does this anger feel like in my body?
Am I fully prepared to release this anger?

When you're ready to release the anger from your body, get physical. Release it in a way that feels good to you, and if you're comfortable, share your experience in the Phoenix Tribe.

MANTRA

I am safe to feel and release my anger.

MELTDOWNS AND MAGIC
Chapter 13

I often tell my clients to get out of their heads and into their bodies. I say this to help these women not to over think every last task in their lives. The mind is a brilliant vessel, and I am to here to say that listening to it is wrong. In fact, I want you to use your mind, for it is capable of so much. It's wise and powerful beyond anything we can possibly imagine. The problem is, your mind has been screwing you over by keeping you small and making you believe you're not an infinitely powerful being of light and love.

Here is the thing, your mind is like a record player, and you can literally switch the record it plays by observing what the record is in the first place. When we are tuned in, we can really see and observe the messages our mind plays.

Let's be real here for a hot minute. We can't decide all of a sudden to get out of our heads, when for the majority of our lives, we have been all up in our heads. They are the home of our identity and the home of our fear. Getting out of our heads and into our bodies is a process of adding more into the equation and not taking away. I don't want you to let go of your thoughts, rather, I want you to add in more empowering thoughts that will serve you on your journey. When you do this and you infuse your mind with thoughts aligned with your higher self, the thoughts of self-sabotage don't feel as good in your body, so we start making better choices based on power rather than force.

Ultimately, you need your mind to break free from the fight you have with yourself. You need it to logically process and rearrange many of the thoughts holding you back from healing. This will come, soon this will be easy, and your mind will be on your team. You'll be working as one, which empowers you to transform and transcend. So let's not shame the mind; let's not let go of the thoughts. Embrace them. Be curious out them. Do anything but justify them.

The soul is where the mind and body connect. Remember the Venn diagram I talked about in Chapter 7? The soul is in the middle where the mind and body connect. It's the place that feels the most natural to us. That divine place is home to the truth of who we are at our deepest level. Our soul is the profound knowing. The soul doesn't question and second guess. It just decides what it wants, without justification or explanation.

Your soul doesn't crave double chocolate ice cream at 2:30 am when nobody's watching you. Your soul doesn't throw insults at you that make you question your worth. Your soul is pure love, and what is good for your soul is good for the world.

Emotions don't need to be explained or justified. When we feel a certain way, and we act on it, our mind needs to explain why we are making that decision. It's almost as if we need to justify it to make others feel better: "I'm going to leave, because it's getting late, and I have to get up early, and there is going to be traffic on the way home." You want to leave – that is it. Enough said. You are allowed to want what you want, just because you want it, for no other reason but because your soul is asking for it.

I am a recovering people pleaser. If there were a 12 Step Program for that, I would be all over it. It was my mission to please others. I was so terrified I wouldn't be liked, so I would go out of my way to make sure someone else's life experience was better than mine so they would respect me and like me. Little did I know, this was actually having the exact opposite affect I wanted.

I would go to parties I didn't want to go to, have conversations that didn't excite me, throw parties just to impress people, and never really let people know how I truly felt about the situation. I would always pride myself on saying that I was super easy going, when really, I just didn't have much of a voice and was scared of rejection. I created a cage around myself, and I didn't let myself feel fully expressed and open, because I was terrified I would upset others.

When you are a people pleaser, you attract takers. You attract those certain kinds of people (we all know the kind) who have an interest in seeing what they can get out of you, and you give in, because you're afraid of what they will think of you otherwise. When you are a people pleasure, you're always giving from an empty cup. You keep giving, so people continue to expect you to give, and then they resent you when you can't give any more, because you just don't have anything left for them, let alone yourself.

It's time to use your voice and let the world know what you want. When you suppress what you want, you rob the world of your soul. This is not only harmful and damaging; it's purely selfish to the world. You are essentially saying to your soul, "You're not good enough to be heard, so shut up. I got this."

As I was recovering from being a people pleaser, one of my mentors said, "What is good for you is good for the world." Essentially, whatever it is you want, voice it and act on it. This task is easier said than done, especially as a recovering people pleaser.

What is good for you is good for the world.

Like anything, you need to start small. When you can listen to what your body wants and act on its desires, you start to build trust. The more trust you build within yourself, the better it feels and the more confidence you have as a result. Asking for what you want is like a muscle: the more you exercise it, the stronger it will be to ask for what you want and follow through on it. When our soul is suppressed because we don't ask for what we want, we turn to food to feed our emotions rather than releasing them.

Perhaps you've been disconnected from your soul for years, and the thought of being in tune with it seems like a daunting and damn near impossible task. I get it. We are so inundated with "things" and "stuff" that keep us disconnected from our souls and from what we truly want. This is awesome for any company trying to sell something. They can then sell us stuff we don't need and make a killing doing it. When we are disconnected from our soul, we aren't in tune with what we really need at a core level. We think we know (and try to feed it with food and "stuff") but really, we have no idea. We need to give ourselves space to listen and get curious.

That means space from social media, space from people, and space from anything that takes your attention away from the present moment. What's one of the most common responses to someone asking, "How are you?" No matter how they really are, people will respond, "Oh my God! I'm so busy!"

It's like a badge of honour people wear. But, here is the truth: the majority of the things that are keeping people busy are manufactured tasks they are doing so they don't have to feel their emotions and listen to their soul. So, "I'm so busy!" is a perfect way to let the world know how important they are. You're either one of these kinds of people, or you know someone who wears this badge of honour.

When we are "busy" we don't have space to transform. Space is a beautiful thing - when we calm down, life sorts itself out. Your body has a way of organizing the things that are pressing to you, and when you relax and just allow, magical things happen. Yes, you'll feel pain. Yes, you'll want to grab your phone and scroll Instagram. Yes you'll want to run and dive head first into Netflix and a bag of chips. The need for distraction will feel like a painful pull, and your ego will try and defend itself, but the more you sit in the pain and feel though it, the more access you will have to your soul.

I can assure you that when you are on your deathbed, you won't be wishing that you made more of an effort to please more people or be distracted from truly listening to your soul. You won't lie there thinking, "If only I use food to numb the emotion I was feeling a little more so I didn't get to know myself. I wish I just binged a little more on those Oreos, because fuck, those were so good."

No, you won't be thinking any of that. But, you will likely regret not becoming the highest, best, and most authentic version of yourself you could possibly be.

You are reading this book because you're on this beautiful path of self-discovery and growth. You have this book in your hands, because you're on a mission to become the highest, best, and most authentic version of yourself. Give yourself the gift of space, the gift of presence, and the gift of exploration.

Eventually you'll get to explore the edges of your soul and be a curious observer to the magic that is life. We never know how much pain we can feel or how much happiness we can handle until we allow ourselves to explore these edges – allow ourselves to fall deeply into our pain, knowing we have the ability to handle it and release it.

Be the observer.
Be the child of your own universe.
Be the warrior who feels the pain.
Be the explorer.
Be the love.

When we can shift from being at war with what we want into truly acknowledging, honouring, and acting on it, we begin to establish a new connection with our soul. Our soul finally realizes that it's being heard. It will begin to speak louder and clearer as it knows you're listening, creating a beautiful bond between your mind and your body.

Mind and body were designed to work in harmony together, as one - not to be at war with one another. You know that feeling when you have when two of your friends are battling it out? You can literally cut the tension with a knife. They fight hard, each believing she is "right." You know that super awkward, stressful situation? Imagine that, but in your body, happening each and every moment of your life. It's a silent battle between your soul and your fear.

Now imagine for a moment you were to speak the words of this battle out loud and put a voice to the voices battling in your head. Imagine the chaos! We all know that initial calling of the soul, our soul voice it's so subtle we can barely put an identity to it. As soon as it arises, our mind interprets right away to tell us why the decision is wrong, or irresponsible, or not the right one. Then we go back and forth for ages, increasing the inner chaos and frustration.

Soul: "Quit your job. You're miserable!
Go pursue your dream."

Fear: "You're an idiot! You are so in debt. That's a stupid idea."

Soul: "You are designed for more. That fire in your belly?
Yeah, that needs to be expressed."

Fear: "But, my job isn't terrible all of the time.
At least I have a job."
Soul: "Take a chance. Trust me
– I've got you."

Fear: "But what if I fail?!?!"

It's incredibly hard to follow your heart and soul when your fear is taking center stage. It's hard to listen and honour the call when we are riddled with doubt. As you begin to listen to your soul, it's important to note that the thoughts of your mind are simply trying to keep you safe.

When we settle in and just listen to the soul, it's relaxing, it's calming, it feels right, and it feels aligned. Why? Because this is your higher self communicating to you. It knows best. This battle is not exclusive to career moves, of course. In fact, this is a similar conversation that takes place when we are on the verge of binge eating.

Fear: "There is ice cream in the fridge. I feel terrible, I need it, I
      deserve it, I need to change how I feel!"

Soul: "It's not what I need."

Fear: "I'm going to eat it all, and then tomorrow I will
 start my diet. I promise I will diet tomorrow."

Soul: In times like this, the soul is so muffled you can't hear it. When I didn't trust myself, my fear was on full volume – it was raging, and my soul could barely get a word in edgewise. This put me in a state of hypnosis. I felt like I was being controlled by the powerful thoughts of my mind. It's important in these places we settle into the voice and the pain.

Pain is one of our greatest teachers, and it's truly a catalyst for growth. When we give into our fear, and we decide that the only option is to numb our emotions with food, we deny ourselves an incredible opportunity for growth. Pain is simply a divine teacher that we need to become the highest, best, and most authentic versions of ourselves.

When we can feel the pain and gain knowledge from it, then we can begin to transcend and heal – we can use it to become who we really are.

What is pain really communicating to us? It's saying we are living under the potential of who we are. It's telling us that something is out of whack. Essentially, we are out of alignment with the highest, best, and most authentic versions of ourselves.

Food will never fill the gaping hole in your soul. It's a battle you will never win. You will never find freedom in filling your soul with food. It will drive you deep into a diet depression where you think food is the answer and always ignore where the love needs to flow. When we allow love to flow into the parts of ourselves that need it we can truly set ourselves free. When we can effectively change the relationship we have to pain, we can change our lives for the better. We can push through the battles and learn to use them as the catalysts to our own healing.

For years of my life, I hated pain. I feared it. I was totally pain adverse in every way, especially emotionally. I numbed the pain I felt in my body with food, social media, exercise, anything. It was too much to bear.

However, I have been able to change my relationship to emotional pain in such a profound way. My journey navigating my threshold for emotional pain was, and continues to be, an interesting and exhilarating journey. Settling into it and sitting with it feels like I am on drugs. It feels as if I'm setting into unknown territory that I shouldn't be in, as if I'm doing something wrong. Which makes perfect sense, because for the majority of my life, I told myself that it was "bad" to feel pain, so I didn't. I would just numb it or suppress it.

Even from a very young age, I avoided pain. When I came last in a dance competition or I didn't book a role that I auditioned for seven times, I just forgot about it, suppressed it, and moved on, setting my eyes on the next thing. I spiritually bypassed my pain and forgot about it immediately. I powered though, being the headstrong and stubborn child I was.

When I'm working with my clients, I often refer to the idea of "sitting in the shit." The phrase is self-explanatory – you literally need to sit right in the emotional shit. You know that feeling? That sticky, terrible, heavy-hearted feeling? Yes, that one. Sit in that. Sit in it until it begins to diminish. Be with it – all of it. It's important to give pain a voice and an identity. Speak it out. Speak to your pain. Using statements that start with "I feel" is a beautiful way to put the pain into words:

I feel a heaviness in my heart.
I feel like I'm going to throw up.
I feel like punching a wall.
I feel like I'm worthless.
I feel like I am not lovable.

Whatever comes out is perfect, because that is your truth. The goal here is to break down the barriers and find your truth of who you are. The pain is a messenger, and it's there to show us the gap between how we are living now and who we are at the highest level. Anxiety and pain are simply messengers to let us know something is out of alignment with our higher selves.

Think of it like two horizontal lines. The top line represents your highest self, where you're at when everything is working for you, when your actions originate from love. The bottom line is where you are at currently. Pain intersects when those lines are too far apart, and the goal is to shorten the space between the two. When we get closer and closer to our highest selves, life truly becomes easy. Life is supposed to be easy. If we are struggling, something is out of alignment.

A lot of my work revolves around the concept of micro decisions. You see, it can be overwhelming as hell to wake up with the intentions of becoming our higher selves, especially if, for the last few years (decades?) of our lives, we have been living out of alignment. Micro decisions are an easy way to observe our actions and behaviours. It's a simple question of "Am I going towards, or further away from my highest self?"

These are small, seemingly insignificant decisions that you make on a daily basis that bring you either closer or further away from your higher self. This is the power of the compound effect. When we look at the results of our lives, it's a compound effect of many, many decisions made over a number of years. Some of the decisions we make each day we've made so many times, so the answers are so ingrained in us we don't even realize there's another option. We follow through on this action because it serves us at some level. It doesn't mean it serves our higher self, but it can serve our ego, so we can become addicted to the decision.

For instance, self-sabotage is a decision you've made. It's something you've done for years and continue to do because it's so ingrained in you. Every single time you decide to talk smack about yourself, you are distancing yourself from your higher self. Every time you decide to overeat, you are distancing yourself.

The cost of distancing from your higher self is huge. When we can bring awareness to our little decisions and shift them, we can change the trajectory of our lives. Think of all the decisions you may have made today already.

Should I meditate today?
Should I drink this glass of water?
Should I have this ice cream?
Should I work out?
Should I suppress that emotion?
Should I ignore that pain?

The majority of them are routine — you've always made them, so you continue to act on them. What decisions could you have made differently? If you brought awareness to the situation, would you make a different decision?

You are the creator. You decide.

PRACTICE IN ACTION

Awareness is a beautiful thing. Once we are aware of our patterns, beliefs, and behaviours, we have the power to transform and transcend them. Without this awareness, we are numb to knowing how our behaviors affect our lives. Awareness of the difference between the fear voice and the soul voice is absolutely critical. Our souls, our bodies, our intuition know best. The answer is always there. Our souls always have our back, no matter what. It's essential that you can decipher between the fear "yes" or "no" that comes from the mind and the soul "yes" or "no" that comes from the body.

When presented with the same exercise I'm about to ask you to do, one of my clients said to me, "But Sam, my soul voice said I wanted the chocolate cake!"

That is a great story, but it's truly not the case. You can consciously choose to treat yourself to a piece of chocolate cake, while being completely present and deciding in advance that you are not going to shame yourself after the fact. However, your body will never scream for sugar – that my friend, is the mind.

EXERCISE #13

This exercise is all about questioning your body and mind and observing where the answer is coming from. Is the answer your body's response or your mind's response? It's important to ask these questions out loud. Vocalize the questions then simply observe the answer your body is giving you.

If when you ask yourself the question and you immediately start to get into negotiation, that is your mind responding.

You: "Am I hungry?"

Body: "Yes, let's eat."

Mind: "Wait, but the number on the scale was higher this morning. You didn't work out today."

Body: "But I'm hungry."

Mind: "Doesn't matter."

The voice of your mind is more familiar to you, because it's been screaming at you for years. The mind must be quiet to hear the whisper of the body, and this takes a high level of presence.

Throughout your day, ask your body questions. Get clear on the difference between your body "yes", body "no," mind "yes," and mind "no." When we can be the observer of these sensations and conversations in our minds and bodies, we create space. When we become present and create space, we give ourselves the time to make the decision that is most aligned with our highest self, rather than making a decision from a place of compulsion. If you are feeling numb to the body voice, ask yourself how you can be more present. Accept your busy mind. Don't fight it. What you fight will strengthen, so be ok with the thoughts and allow them to come and go until you're in the moment and can hear your body's voice clearly.

MANTRA

I am in the process of fully trusting my intuition.

THE BEGINNING

This is not the end. You are rising like the phoenix you are.

The beautiful thing about this work is when we have awareness, we have the ability to transform. When we are left in the dark, there is no light to see the shifts that we need to make in our lives. By virtue of you completing this journey, you now have the divine responsibility to shed all that is not serving you and create space for things aligned with your highest, best, and most authentic self.

Now is the time for divine integration – to fully integrate the practices from the book into your life so you can see lasting change. This work is a journey, and it will continue to be as long as you're committed to the path of growth.

You're safe to feel, to express, and to heal. You're safe to accept, love, and honour yourself, for this is the birthplace of true, sustainable transformation. You were designed for greatness. Underneath all the stories, false identities, and fears is a beacon of pure light and love.

Throughout this journey, you've been asked to rise and challenge the parts of you that are no longer serving you and to love parts of you that you previously ran from and suppressed. This was a beautiful undertaking. You've lit your soul on fire and experienced the feeling of inner self love. You can't unlearn this; you can only deepen it. Each day, you have the ability to deepen this inner love to become more connected to your body and your soul. Thank you for giving yourself this precious gift.

You now hold the light to activate other souls, to show them their way home, back into their bodies. You now have the divine responsibility to be the light, emulate love, and allow others to be drawn into your light. It's contagious, it's raw, and it's real. Being fully connected to our truth is magnetic.

Thank you from the bottom of my heart and soul for taking a chance on me, the work, and yourself. It lights my soul on fire to know you are committed to your growth and you've allowed me to be your guide on your path back home.

I want to continue to support you through this journey, so if you have any questions at all please reach out to support@hungyforhappiness.com, and I will do my best to answer each email I receive. You can also tag me in a post in the Global Community, where I support my tribe of phoenixes on a daily basis.

This is not the end. This is only the beginning.

Welcome to the tribe.

I love you,
Samantha

hungryforhappiness.com/tribe

ABOUT THE AUTHOR

Samantha Skelly is an entrepreneur, motivational speaker, best-selling author, and emotional eating expert. As a leading authority on disordered eating and body image issues, Samantha has made it her life's mission to empower women to overcome their struggles with food and their bodies so they can live happy, authentic, and fulfilling lives.

In 2014, Samantha founded Hungry for Happiness, a movement to support women around the world who battle disordered eating and body image issues. Hungry for Happiness provides accessible and affordable recovery resources to those suffering in silence. Through her program, Samantha has revolutionized the weight loss industry by challenging the "Band-Aids for bullet wounds" methodology that has long been the industry standard. She works with clients to examine the individual and underlying causes of eating disorders, and in doing so, she has transformed the lives of countless women around the world by helping them conquer their food and body related issues.

Author of the recent best-seller, Hungry for Happiness: One Woman's Guide From Fighting Food to Finding Freedom, Samantha continues to spread her message and inspire thousands of people through her program, worldwide international retreats, motivational speaking engagements, and the Hungry for Happiness podcast. Samantha has had the privilege of sharing her mission on an international platform, with appearances on Global TV, Shaw, NBC, and, CBC. In 2013, Samantha was awarded "Top 24 under 24" by 24 hrs Vancouver, and in 2014, she was named a finalist for "Best Emerging Entrepreneur" by Small Business BC.

A native of Vancouver, British Columbia, Samantha currently resides in San Diego, California. She supports initiatives that aim to prevent and stop human trafficking and donates a portion of Hungry for Happiness profits to help rescue and rehabilitate trafficking victims in Cambodia and North America.

When she's not challenging the weight loss industry or transforming lives, Samantha can usually be found indulging in tacos, playing on slip and slides, or pole dancing.

10289272R00112

Made in the USA
San Bernardino, CA
28 November 2018